Happy Departures

Towards Significant Life

notionpress.com

HAPPY DEPARTURES

Towards Significant Life

ARVIND AGRAWAL

notionpress.com

Notion Press

Old No. 38, New No. 6

McNichols Road, Chetpet

Chennai - 600 031

First Published by Notion Press 2015

ISBN: 978-93-52061-68-6

Neutrality Disclaimer:

Though this book is written in the 'he' narrative, it is only to facilitate easy and fluid reading. The author suggests reading it with a 'she' wherever appropriate. He disclaims any bias whatsoever for any gender in this work.

Buyers and readers of the book also agree with the standard disclaimers regarding the outcome of use of the ideas and opinions suggested in this book. The author, editors, publishers, distributors, agents and even the readers taking the initiative to form the 'Significant Group' mentioned throughout this book are not liable for any unsolicited and unexpected outcome.

Dedicated to the Infinity that is within us and within which we are…

Advance Acclaims For *Happy Departures*

"A good book that help you and improve your faith in yourself to travel the journey of life with a smile even when the conditions don't seem to be favourable.

This book will give precisely what you need: hope, strength, clarity, energy, direction and focus."

- ABHAY TARE

Managing Director, Apex Pools Pvt. Ltd., Indore, India

"A practical book on the psychology of transformation…"

- CHIUNG-WEI HUANG

Lecturer, Chien Hsin University of Science and Technology, Jhongli, Taiwan

"Very insightful and thoughtful… The design and flow of the book get the point home, and to the heart."

- HARSHA MUKHERJEE

Managing Director, International Institute of CSR, Mumbai, India

"The principles and techniques of forgiveness and living a Significant Life; and how these virtues manifest to personal contentment from moment to moment - these have been very well brought up in this book."

- J P MENON,

Vice President, St. Marks Hotel, Bangalore, India

"A fantastic read and workbook to live with purpose; insightful read on being here and now… Brings awareness on how to live with joy and purposefulness…"

- KASSIE GOUNDEN

Pat Gounden & Co. (Professional Accounting firm), Shallcross, South Africa

"This is a truly groundbreaking book. Dr. Agrawal combines a mastery of psychology with a real knack for exploring the purpose and transformation of life to do nothing less than lay the groundwork for a new, powerful, mind-brain approach.

Even if you don't practice feedback on self-awareness; the treasure of precious insights in this book so deepens your appreciation of the brain-heart interaction, that you can't help but be changed by this truly wonderful and insightful book.

A must-read for everyone…"

- KARTIK PANDYA

Director (Operations), Indus University, Ahmedabad, India

"This wonderful book is full of wisdom and important life lessons for success. The book is loaded with great ideas that will help you live a more meaningful life; a life designed around a purpose.

Equally useful for budding entrepreneurs who will find the final chapter very useful because they need to manage the 'fear' factor on day-to-day basis; and also because they ought to be driven by a *reason* and a sense of *purpose* today, more than ever before; by the change they wish to bring, rather than the profit motives alone…"

- MANOJ NAIR

International Contracts Consultant & Coach

"Arvind has been my longtime friend; he always appeared too curious which kept him seeking. The result of his spirit of seeking, presented here in form of this book, is miraculous. Simple set of questions in this work *Happy Departures* are the ones; amazingly placed in a proper context, which one can accept or reject but can't ignore in concurrent times when we are faced with duality between what *we want to have* and *what we want to do*.

A comprehensive help for many of us, finally!"

- SANDEEP SABHARWAL

Founder Director, Indian School of Development Foundation, Navi Mumbai, India

"Dramatically straight-forward, meaningful and timely; this book has arrived just in time. We have been so much in search of purpose, but we were lost in our profession.

Perhaps the only book on work-life balance... A must-read for every age-group."

- SHYAM SHARMA

President (HR & Corporate Communications), Claris Lifesciences Ltd., Ahmedabad, India

"Dr Arvind has carefully and diligently brought up all the questions and inhibitions most of us live with, the ones that diminish our spirit of living life to its fullest. Thankfully, he also provides techniques and solutions. I am now convinced that human society collectively has to still go a long way on true development, a phase of development that cannot be accomplished through technology."

- VINAY JOSHI CHANDNIWALA (PhD)

Associate Professor, Jagran Lakecity University, Bhopal, India

I ACKNOWLEDGE WITH GRATITUDE...

The values I received from my *gurus*, mentors and teachers that guided me through my education, career and business.

All the books, people and events that touched my life, making me the way I am today.

The tolerance and unconditional love I received from my parents, my wife's parents, my brothers and sisters, and my friends who accepted me the way I was and helped me get better.

The patience of my wife and two sons who allowed me my space to experiment with life.

The information I have gained from countless books, websites, articles, blogs, quotations and talks.

A very special thanks to Matthew O'Reilly for his prompt and kind permission to refer his TED talk in this book

The phenomenal work put in by the entire team at Notion Press that brought to life this work.

Contents

INTRODUCTION

How will this book help me?

My curious mind had been probing a simple question for many years: *Why is it that when most of us seem intelligent, ambitious and smart, our levels of accomplishments and contentment vary*? I have found that sense of accomplishment is anchored to two common factors: (1) Level of clarity in understanding and comprehension (2) Organising life around a purpose.

More the clarity about the purpose, higher the accomplishments. In this book, we will discuss how to develop clarity about the purpose.

How do we ever identify the *purpose* of life? Is there a 'technique' for it? *Who am I* and *what am I here for;* these questions have usually been asked in spiritual realms and discourses because they are too abstract to be given a thought in our normal course of living. For most of us, these are either not the right set of questions or 'now' is not the right time to address these questions.

As my search continued, I found a dramatically different *technique* that is not as abstract, one that lies at the cross-section of self-help and self-search and one which can remarkably accelerate our personal and professional progress.

We have been scared of death for thousands of years now. We have conquered the deadliest oceans, mountains, and all kinds of challenges that time and nature could present. Despite facing many challenges, why do we fear death?

Are we living with the 'correct theories' about death? How can we ever reach a theory that everyone agrees with, regardless of one's faith and level of accomplishment? Many may discard the inputs from the spiritual domain for lack of sufficient proof, but what about the hundreds of others who have 'experienced' death? (Study of NDE or near-death-experience is slowly becoming an independent branch of scholarly research.) Such people report a definite internal transformation, a sense of purpose, clarity, compassion and love beyond their own normal expectations, capacity or imagination.

Imagine the world full of such people: purposeful, clear, compassionate and loving. What will humanity be if each one of us can somehow undergo a similar transformation? The experience of others must translate into 'awareness' for everyone. Each of us does not need to go through this experience personally; we can go by that of others.

Have I ever had a near-death experience? Never! Did I experience the fear of death? Never!! (Though life did come very 'close' to me time and again, many times in all these years, so much that I can almost say that if life were something tangible, I have almost 'touched' it.) I have presented, with full awareness, the correlation between four sets of ideas that have been away and apart from each other. The four sets of knowledge are (1) research in the domain of near-death and trans-death experiences (2) our own understanding of the utility of life (3) our expectations from life and (4) the available explanation of the phenomenon called life.

These four bodies of knowledge have stayed away and apart. The distance has been due to two factors. I will call them the boundaries of the expert *(I will stay within my area of expertise)* and the learners' boundaries *(I will not explore)*. This book becomes relevant when we drop these boundaries and allow some overlapping.

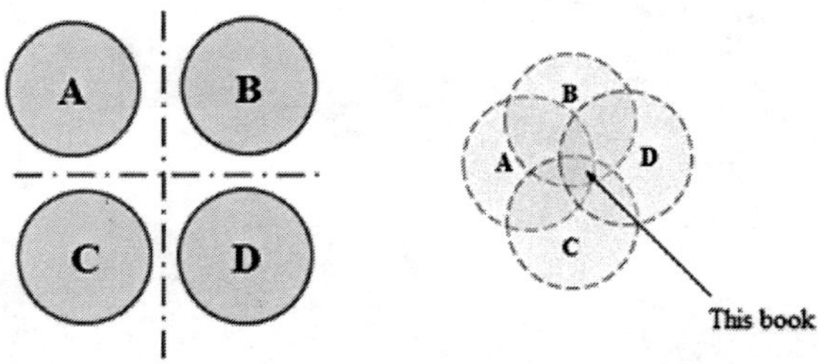

A	Research in domain of near-death and trans-death experiences
B	Our own understanding of the utility of life
C	Our expectations from life
D	Available explanations about the phenomenon called life
— · —	Expert's boundary
——	Learner's boundary

The result may appear slightly weird or like *work-in-progress*. All the fine things of today were once weird or resembling work-in-progress, like this first airplane.

Through this book, I have compiled and presented ideas based on others' experiences, research and explanations, combined with my reflective and curious commentary to make it a proposition that can be put to application.

This book is an initiative to examine the patterns of our awareness about what life is, what death is, and, more importantly, what is the utility of both. Discovering the utility of both involves internal reorientation, and in that sense this book is a 'practical handbook' of 'transformation psychology'; *how one does one change from within?*

The backdrop is equally fascinating: we are moving to 'knowledge society' and further to 'wisdom society' (We moved from 'information age to 'knowledge society' quite rapidly; we shall not take too long to move to 'wisdom society' where the source of awareness will be not the information, not the theoretical text, but the systematic and slow but perpetual reflection; where the 'status-symbol' may reduce to 'symbol of ignorance')

Did you know that most of us never **accept** (to ourselves) or **express** (to others) that we are not satisfied with what we have, what we do, or what we are? Purposefulness and *what do I want* are the two sides of the same coin.

Let me tell how this book will help.

If you are a young reader, it will help you identify or get a glimpse of the purpose of your career, if not entire life. Without this clear direction, people land on space after 10-15 years feeling this is not what they wanted. This book can save you many years.

If you are a reader in the middle of your career, you will find strokes that will bring a balance between the personal and professional spheres. The abrasion between the two, I know, creates plenty of heat and stress. You will be able to seek your way out if you ever felt this is not what you wanted.

If you are a respected elderly reader and if life had pushed a few heartbreaking moments your way (which it usually does), causing regret that this was not what you had wanted, then you will find techniques to 'detox' yourself, if I may say so. You may arrive at the point of contentment and be able to bless more people more often. On the other hand, if life has treated you well, you will find an echo of your inner voice throughout this book.

The theme of the book is such that a reader will need lots of 'personal space'. Hence, due care has been taken in this regard while creating the internal layout of the book giving ample space for readers to jot down their thoughts and ideas. Readers will find several illustrations that will enable the comprehension of the subject matter and several questions to help reflect upon discussions.

You will find sufficient space and opportunities in this book to make it your personal diary. In fact, all the questions you will find in the book are equally important as the text is. These questions are designed to let you engage in a systematic individual or collective introspection and dialogue. It will help co-create a new awareness about the utility of life.

The book is written with a single purpose: the feeling of ambiguity, fear and ominousness linked with death must diminish. *Dar ke aage jeet hai* is a famous Hindi movie dialogue. Only when we get rid of every kind of fear, we can obtain a sense of purposefulness.

The energy and force called life deserves a chance.

Arvind Agrawal

June 2015

1

So that we can write the story of our own life...

We do not remember days, we remember moments.

- Cesare Pavese

All of us reach a moment in life when we ask ourselves what is or what has been the meaning, significance and purpose of our lives. This question is universal. It is not dependent on our lifestyle, religion, citizenship or education.

Finding an answer to this question is essential for the contentment of the self. And this has some significance for others too, because there is a 'hidden' lesson and an insight.

At a deep level, each of us is a child; and as children do, we also learn not from life, but from a story.

Write your own life's story. This idea is powerful. It is not essential that this story is as melodramatic as we are used to watching on a large screen. It could be like any other story in which we are the central character and there is something *very simple* to learn from the story.

Sir Terry Pratchatt, a famous English novelist, once said: "If you don't turn your life into a story, you become part of someone else's story." One may have a really exciting story or, on the other extreme, the story may be incomplete. It does not matter. As long as you have your own story, even being part of a bigger story is fine to some extent. To be left out is the worst scenario. Most times, we have our own story and we are also part of a bigger one. The power is in the story, not in *what* or *who*.

Searching within…

1. What have been the important turns in my life?
2. What have been the obstacles and ironies of my life?
3. How did I handle challenges?
4. What lessons did I take from these events?
5. Who and what kept me inspired during these days?

2

WRITE THE STORY OF YOUR LIFE WITH A GLORIOUS MIND

> *Open your eyes, look within. Are you satisfied with the life you are living?*
>
> **- Bob Marley**

What is that we call 'life'? Is life our family and work? Is life the process of inhaling and exhaling air? Is life all the accomplishments we have gathered? This question is something worth pondering, reflecting upon and discussing.

Our life (with the stress on 'our') may be limited. However, life itself is perpetual and relentless. This brings us back to the question again: What is life?

When we study mythological texts and history, we may conclude that one story is but a part of another bigger story and all the stories are heading towards merging into the one big story. Is there the one story that is eternal and infinite?

Is our life also a story that will merge into the eternal and infinite story? Is our life the body we possess, the breathing, the name we have, the accomplishments? No, no, no!

Our life is pure consciousness - something we call the 'mind' in day-to-day conversation.

We handle this 'mind' ignorantly and carelessly. For an untrained person, the mind is like a garbage bin, full of swirling negative emotions, illusions, fear, aversion, hate, envy, depression, stress, confusion, and desires. And with all these, the mind becomes heavy, cumbrous and gross.

The 'mind' should be glorious and spirited, because it has to travel, travel very long, within this life and beyond.

What we casually call 'mind' is the consciousness. (Later in this book, we will distinguish between the terms 'mind', 'soul', 'spirit' and 'consciousness').

Consciousness is the element because of which life is perpetual. Glorious and spirited consciousness can be our asset, provided we make some efforts to achieve this unique state of mind. And it is not so difficult. With glorious consciousness, the story of our life will be 'different'. It will have both contentment and lessons duly and fully learned.

It is known to brain studies that our existence has three abstract components. The mind, intellect and wit, based at three different parts of the 'brain': at the back, on the top, and on the frontal side, respectively. The mind is the seat of all neutral, positive and negative emotions, the intellect is the base for all logical and analytical processes, and wit is the basis for all judgemental, conclusive and decisive thought processes.

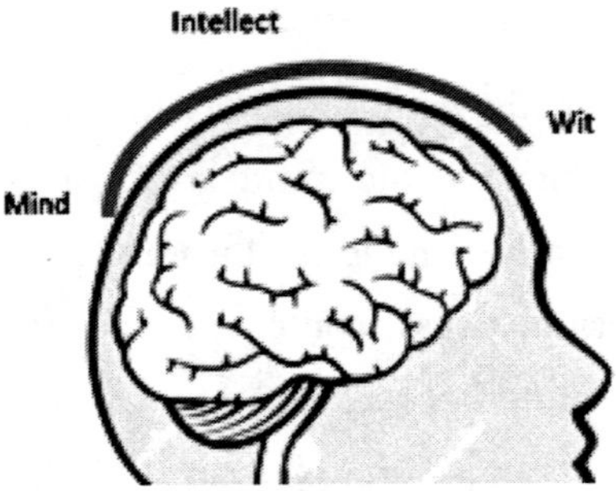

Most of our behaviour is influenced by the intellect and the mind, i.e. at the top and back of the brain. If we can learn to bring our attention to the wit and talk, act and behave in a far-sighted manner, then our 'story' is going to be different. The story can be profound if we begin by taking care of our mind, which is ours only – by cleaning it, by clearing it.

A glorious mind does not really need much wit. In fact, it creates one.

Searching within…

1. Can I perceive my mind to be a distinct entity than the body?
2. How is my mind? Am I satisfied with it?
3. What are those five words that describe my mind?
4. Who is accountable for this state of my mind?
5. How is the state of my mind affecting my persona and efficiency?

3

Life is perpetual

> *A baby is God's opinion that life should go on.*
>
> **- Carl Sandburg**

Dr Brian Weiss, Dr Michael Newton and many experts in science accept today that the 'physical shutdown' is not the end of our existence. We come back, with another name, with another body, in another city, born into a family that speaks another language, in the next three months or 300 years.

Life and consciousness are in perpetual flow. It is the limitation of our mind if we cannot accept this or figure out its rules and directions.

Perpetuity of life: What do we have to do with that? We need to be concerned because within this single life can we get all the resources and opportunities required to control the quality of life in this and the next trip? What is required is a cleansing of the mind. Consciousness and life are two sides of the same coin and both are perpetually moving.

Hard to believe, isn't it? If we cannot believe, we can at least wonder that we are going to return with the same mind or the same consciousness. Psychologists have recorded hundreds of cases where clients have shared accounts of their experiences between lives and how, during the gap between lives, the 'review' of the previous life happens. They have also recorded information regarding the way clients are coached and corrected and how they used their 'free will' and took a decision to come back again. This field of awareness is gradually developing as an independent 'science'.

We can continue to wonder about this till we reach the state of belief.

Our understanding of life and the nature of life (including our opinion about its perpetuity) is influenced by two factors: our religious values and our scientific temperament. There are only two possibilities in general. One either believes in the perpetuity of life (reincarnation) or does not. Let us call these possibilities A and B, respectively. Remember, both the opinions are quite personal in nature and are not verifiable with the tools and techniques of science and statistics as we know so far. Both the possibilities should raise curiosity.

- Case A: if there is perpetuity in life, what happens next, what happens in between two lives?
- Case B: If there is only one life, what is the best use of it?

This book is not designed to give any readymade conclusive answers, it is designed to stir new questions.

Searching within...

1. Have I read *Messages from the Masters*?
2. Have I ever clearly experienced within the family, neighbourhood or relatives that one of our great grandparents has come back as a newborn child?
3. We are what life is or is life what we are?
4. Am I able to estimate the oneness, power and perpetuity of life and consciousness?
5. What is holding me from accepting the possibilities of life beyond this life?

4

STAY HAPPY

> *I have told my children that when I die, release balloons in the sky to celebrate that I graduated. For me, death is a graduation.*
>
> **- Elisabeth Kulber-Ross**

When do we feel happy? Don't we feel happy when 'everything' is happening the way we 'thought' it should? Thoughts! That 'mind' has come back to the discussion.

After all, where do we fix our mind? Where *should* we fix it? Whenever the mind is fixated and everything seems to be alright, the mind becomes happy. The question is: Where do we fixate the mind?

Where should we fix our mind? On the travel tickets, on the travel itself, or on what the travel is meant to accomplish?

The mind as such is 'innocent'. It gets stuck wherever we fix it.

If we fix the mind on petty things, we get small pleasures. If one fixes it on temporary things, he will get temporary happiness. The travel ticket is very temporary; it loses its value once the travel is over. If we fix the mind on petty and temporary stuff, the happiness we derive will also be small and temporary.

The mind has two qualities: (1) it needs to get stuck somewhere and (2) it wants to be happy.

If, at the moment of departure, the mind is not happy, the next part of the trip may begin with a heavy mind.

So, stay happy. Every moment. At any cost.

Searching within…

1. Have I ever trained myself to stay happy?
2. What do we need to stay happy?
3. Where does my mind swing or get stuck?

   Mostly ______________________

   Usually ______________________

   At times ______________________
4. Do I control my mind or does my mind control me?
5. When I am happy, how do I feel, what do I do?

5

EACH DAY IS ONE DAY CLOSER TO THE NEXT LIFE

If you love life, don't waste time, for time is what life is made up of.

- Bruce Lee

It is in our basic nature to make comparisons. It is fine to take the support of this faculty because it enhances the way we understand our surroundings.

If we compare the lives of all the people we know, we can do a classification based on two factors: (a) what is more: pain or happiness and (b) the level of awareness which can be either low or high. Going by such classification, life can be one of the following four kinds.

Happy	Ignorant-Happy	Wise-Happy
Suffering	Ignorant-Suffering	Wise-Suffering
	Ignorant	Wise

It is but natural that all of us want to lead a wise and happy life.

Now, let us explore two aspects.

- How do we move from ignorance towards awareness?
- What are the patterns of continuity of our lives?

Take ignorance first. To sharpen and make the intellect useful, we need to do something.

"There is something that I do not know, something that I need to understand." This is the starting point.

We need to open up our mind, push the ego away, and submit ourselves to someone who is definitely more knowledgeable than we are. We have to gain experience, read books, reflect upon what we know (or do not know), get involved in discussions and debates, and shift the mind from entertainment to other learning-oriented engagements for some time. You may recall that the mind wants to get fixated somewhere and remain happy there. The challenge is to get the mind fixed on something. That's it!

As far as the question of suffering-happiness is concerned, there are two factors – perception and *ḳarma.*

- **Perception**: This largely depends on us whether we are happy or unhappy. Factors and circumstances are outside us. But the feelings of suffering and happiness are inside us. In fact, these feelings are part of us. Perception is in a way the angle with which we see and understand the outside factors. Only by changing this angle, new meanings start appearing. And to let that happen, what we need the most is cooperation with the self. We may not have ears for others' suggestions as they sound like empty orations.

- The principles and effects of ***karma*** are slightly complex and strikingly interesting. (If you are leading a *Significance Group** (these are off-line groups conceptualised to discuss and implement the concepts, questions and actions recommended in this book), please do read and have a discussion on the book titled *Theory of Karma* by Heera Bhai Thakkar.)

These principles in summary: (1) *Karma* is like a seed. Some seeds germinate and bear fruits quickly, while some take longer. (2) Good *karma* results in good fortune, bad *karma* yields bad fortune. (3) *Karma* is not the result of what we do with our physical organs alone. Even *intention* leads to *karma*. (Then there is a fourth principle which we will explore in discussion 18.)

Going by these principles, we can infer that today's happiness is connected with some past *karma* and today's sufferings and miseries are due to some bad *karma* of the past. Extending this further, to enjoy happiness in the present and the future, we need to accumulate good *karma* (like an investment).

---

* To undertake training for Significance Group formation and leadership, please visit http://www.addwit.org/significance-group/ or send an email to significancegroup@gmail.com

The patterns of continuity of lives are of four kinds.

Network Pattern 1 (Linear): Life is a straight line. However slow its pace may be, we are progressing towards a better quality of life at the next opportunity (of having life). With experience, we gain wisdom and this wisdom becomes a part of our consciousness. Thus, we begin the journey of our next life with the slightly wiser consciousness.

Network Pattern 2 (Circular): If our *ḳarma* is not sufficiently good, then retrogression is possible, leading to increased suffering. This may form a circular pattern and take the next few lives for recovery.

Network Pattern 3 (Zig-zag): This is a combination of patterns one and two. A person swings like a pendulum between ignorance and wisdom, indulging in all sorts of *ḳarma* (both good and bad). He keeps going back and forth in the flow of lives.

Network Pattern 1

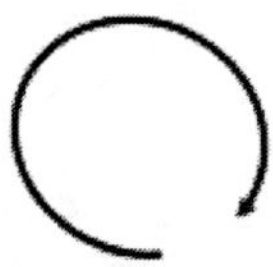

Network Pattern 2

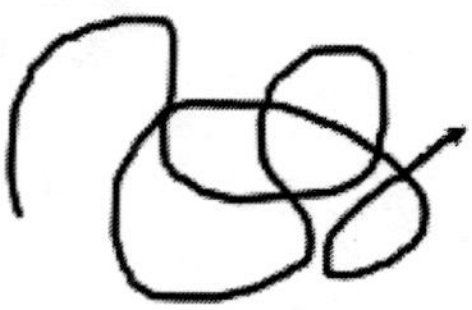

Network Pattern 3

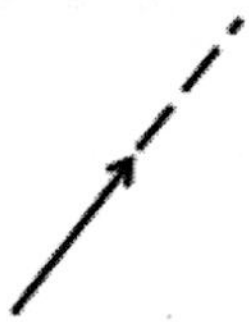

Network Pattern 4

Network Pattern 4 (Command): This is a unique state when one has control over whether to come back in the next life (in the physical body) or not. People with this capacity are called *siddha* (accomplished advanced souls).

So, what is the fundamental issue? Why and how are we closer to the next life each day?

Life is the time available with us. How are we utilising this time? Are we gathering useful wisdom? Are we sowing the seeds of good *karma*? Wisdom influences the quality of our thoughts and *karma*, and thoughts purify and distill our actions.

Wisdom and *karma* will have a lasting impact on the quality of our next life and the level of happiness then.

'Next life' does not literally point to one's next life, it may be the next week, next month or next year.

Searching within…

1. Among the four, what is the quality of life that I have now?
2. What are the pearls of wisdom I can claim I have gathered through my own experiences?
3. What are my plans / strategies to increase my level of awareness?
4. Have I attended the workshop based on the book *Theory of Karma* with my Significance Group leader?
5. Am I prepared to put my time to good use?

6

WHEN 'THAT' COMES, LET THE MIND STAY CONTENTED, AT PEACE

Life is what happens while you are busy making other plans.

- John Lennon

Three elements contribute to giving life to this body – time, breath and consciousness. Without these three, the body is but a sack of bones and muscles.

At that moment, we can have slight control only on the consciousness or on the state of consciousness. We will be given an all-new, fresh lease of breath and time, but it is possible that the much required consciousness will be carried forward to the next innings. And the quality of that consciousness will determine the quality of life in the next innings.

Understand this: We deliberately think and talk about all major life processes and events such as education, career, marriage, kids, car and home. Departure is also one such major event that deserves thinking, discussion and meticulous planning.

Getting scared or anxious about death and becoming desperate or weak when the time arrives – these are signs of lack of preparedness. Fear and anxiety make our consciousness weaker. With a weakened consciousness, the quality of life suffers because the source of all energy and inspiration is our conscience; you may have noticed this fact, haven't you?

So let us pay some heed to planning – to stay contented, composed and peaceful, because strong consciousness is the initial capital of our next life.

Searching within…

1. How will I come to know if my consciousness is happy and contented?
2. During which occasions did I feel contentment and peace?
3. When I feel contentment and peace, don't my will power and efficiency shoot up?
4. How can I help others experience this unique state of mind?
5. Some of the *yogic* breathing techniques [*] help us experience and understand the correlation among breath, emotion and consciousness. Have I explored any such options?

7

The gap between this life and the next: We are going to feel much better after cleaning

> *Don't go through life, grow through life.*
>
> **- Eric Butterworth**

If life is continuous and we are going to return, what happens during the gap? Cleaning and cleaning up, the way we wash clothes between two uses.

Am I writing this after experience? No. Maybe I have had many such experiences, but I cannot recall. What is cleaned during the gap?

Researchers are working tirelessly to find what happens beyond life by recording and studying experiences of people who nearly touched death and returned (near-death experience). With technological advances, resuscitation has become common and possible. They are also studying regression to past lives, a technique in psychotherapy involving hypnosis. This is an emotionally sensitive and a para-physical domain where the empirical proof becomes inadequate and even insignificant.

We need to make progress by *exploring* things and *accepting* a few others. (Do watch the documentary based on the *Tibetan Book for the Dead* with the help of a Significance Group leader.)

The air that is coming in and going out of our body is called breath. When pure consciousness departs, the relationship between the body and air ceases to prevail. The body was all powerful and the brain was able to think and judge this and judge that, till the syndication with the breath and consciousness prevailed.

Air around is there, it always will be there. Consciousness is there, it will always be there. Nature is continuously purifying the air. Consciousness is purified by Infinite Wisdom.

What is Infinite Wisdom? It is the source from which all that we know has arrived – science, economics, mathematics, psychology, literature, arts, music and astronomy.

Infinite wisdom is always pure. Some of us either do not understand it or we explain it wrongly or use it wrongly, or both.

Between two lives, Infinite Wisdom 'works' on us, so that ignorance and rigidity reduce to some degree from our consciousness, thereby improving the next life.

Just like a dirty shirt requires hard scrubbing sometimes, similarly if one's consciousness has been bemired with anger, sadness, aversion, longing, eroticism, envy, hate and jealousy, then it needs scrubbing. However, this scrubbing happens at the state of energy (perhaps a much subtle form of energy than the ones we know such as light, electricity, magnetism and sound). It happens painlessly.

There are no hellfire, pans of boiling oil, snakes, scorpions, or hunters like we read in tales.

This cleaning operation works well. You may have noticed how fresh, lively and sparkling life is when consciousness returns in the form of a newborn child.

So, although there is no proof to show, let us open up to the possibility that the consciousness is cleaned up between two lives. (To know more about what happens to the energy that has left the physical body and proceeded ahead, please read books like *Journey of Souls: Case Studies of Life between Lives* by Michael Newton, Ph. D.)

Searching within…

1. Am I able to accept this idea of cleaning of the consciousness?
2. Do I feel that my consciousness needs cleaning up?
3. What do I need to do to stop further dirtying of my consciousness?
4. Am I feeling a bit strange about how the experience of cleaning up may be?
5. Can I discuss this with a few others in a Significance Group?

8

LIFE IS FOR UTILISING WELL. SIX PEOPLE SHOULD JOIN HANDS AND ADOPT A SIGNIFICANT WORK OR PROJECT

I would rather die a meaningful death than live a meaningless life.

Corazon Aquino

We can classify all things around us into two categories: things that the human society has created (such as television, furniture, clothes, toys, vehicles and books) and things that Mother Nature has created (trees, air, soil and life).

We (or some of us) can claim that we know all about what mankind has created but can anyone claim knowing everything about the things created by Mother Nature? We can only produce chips and juice in factories, not the potatoes and oranges!

However, the next statement is surely true: Every creation has a specific purpose, whether created by mankind or nature. The television is meant for entertainment and news, a car is for convenience in commuting, fruits and vegetables are for providing nutrition, and air, soil and water are for ecology to sustain.

What is the utility or purpose of life? The skills and capacities that man is bestowed with indicate three specific uses of human life.

1. To **gather** wisdom and experience.
2. Use this wisdom and experience to **protect** and preserve our dear ones and our ideas.
3. And slowly, move away from 'I-me-mine' and **contribute** to the quality of life of others and the surroundings.

To shortchange any of these three will amount to abuse or under-utilisation of life; an utter waste of something very precious.

The significance of this one life is in making diligent efforts to accomplish all the three purposes. It is never too late for it. *Jab jaage tab savera*. The moment we realise this (open our eyes to the need or reality), that is *the* perfect time to make a beginning.

And this becomes easy when we come into a group. An individual may have all the excitement, but a group has strength.

This suggestion has some depth and thought to it. Earlier, we explored the principles of *karma*. There is an additional dimension to it which we can call *collective karma*. We need not understand it fully but it is not too difficult to comprehend. The two immediate benefits of this suggestion are: (i) we will have a little more mutual trust (we know people but seldom accept them totally) and (ii) we will have a stronger bond when we work together cohesively on a project.

In the world of electronic connections, these two elements are desperately missing: trust and bond.

This approach is based on positive action rather than positive thinking.

Abraham Maslow identified five tiers of human needs – physiological, safety and security, love and belonging, self-esteem and self-actualisation.

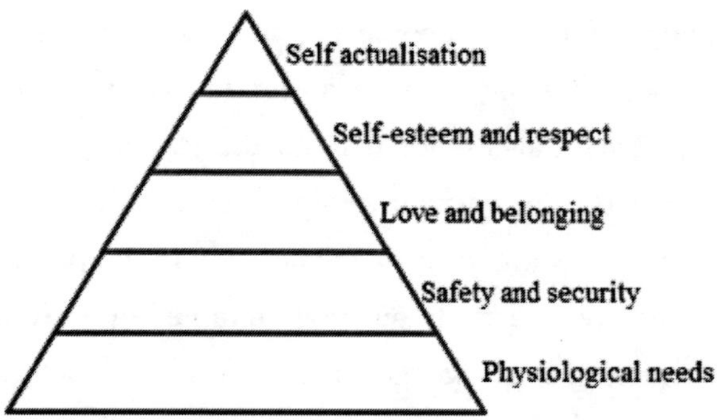

Though most of us progress individually along this hierarchy, a mature person, sooner or later, develops an urge to 'know' the self and the truth (the fifth level). Collectively too, the human society is making progress along the same hierarchy.

Give a thought to this perspective. As soon we realise we have needs, our brain gets pushed forward to finding ways and means to achieving them. For example, how to arrange food and clothes, how to get a secure future, how to get love from others, and how to get respect. Our needs may act like a precursor for enhancing our awareness, and, in due course, with experience, this awareness becomes our wisdom.

Now, it depends on us how do we make progress. Do we get stuck at any level? Will our progress on the journey towards wisdom get stalled? When we seek progress, we seek ways and means for the next level. And this is one of the purposes of life. Our needs are less to do with needs alone, but they are also linked to our inner growth.

More and more people are now keen to understand and explore the significance and meaning of human life. This statement also holds true for the youth, the millennia kids; who do not wish anymore to be caught in rat-race. Ask them; they are keen to engage only in the projects and tasks that have a definite purpose ingrained in it. Today, the collective need of a large section of society is not materialistic, biological and physiological. It is spiritual, with the need for self-actualisation.

In one's life, one may not cross all the five levels. So, the only purpose of life is to move forward from where we left off and ultimately reach (or at least develop an urge for reaching) the stage of having spiritual needs.

What is spiritual need? Spiritual needs are two: (1) attain contentment and joy for the self and (2) then, developing an urge to see others attaining the same contentment and joy.

People who are making earnest and sincere efforts to progress along this hierarchy will enter a state of coordination, solidarity and synergy. This synergy is bound to occur because this is beyond and above the limitations of language, regionalism, religion, nationality and status. Seeking spiritual progress is certainly an individual urge. However, we can also be 'collective seekers'.

Michael Newton writes, "When a soul has led a productive life beneficial to itself and others around it, I notice it returns to the spirit world with enthusiasm."

How do we form a group? Form a small group, not a large one. A group of six is feasible and manageable. There is a suggestion that each in a couple brings along one couple. Thus, three couples form one group. You may also form a group with your close friends.

Should everyone in the group work on the same project or cause? Not necessarily. One may have an inclination towards education, others may have an interest in environment, governance, health or something else.

(In appendix 2, there is a list that will help you identify your inclination. When you have reached a milestone or you are satisfied with what you have been able to do, you may switch your cause or project.)

Remember this: When we are able to do something for others, our mind (which is otherwise bewildered and impatient) attains peace and expanse.

You may also find this one observation handy: the key to be able to do something beyond your comfort zone and still find it fulfilling is 'connectedness', not passion. Let me give an example. Unless I feel 'connected' to trees and nature, I will not find a plantation project fulfilling. Passion, by dictionary definition, is all about intensity, a top-down relationship; whereas 'connectedness' is a linkage, a parallel relationship. I plant trees and plants and take care of them; plants reciprocate by providing fresh air. This logic can be applied to all other projects that you consider.

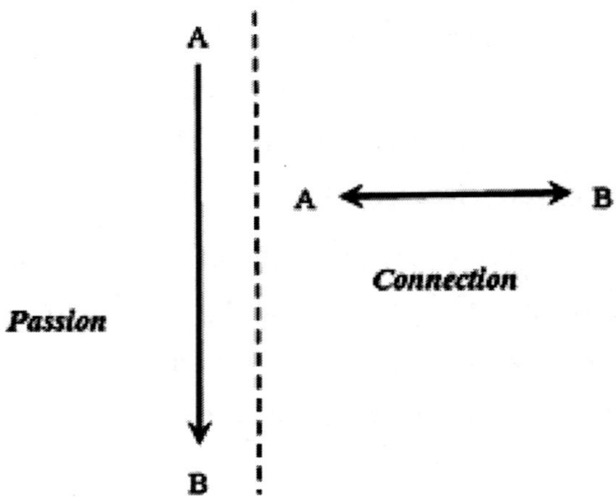

A conscious awareness about connection and reciprocal relationship with those we serve eliminates doer-ship, the *I-ness* which may humanly seep in.

Searching within...

1. Am I prepared to slightly alter the direction of my life and the way it is headed?
2. Am I able to estimate the number of people who will benefit from the experiment I am likely to engage in?
3. Have I ever experienced the strength of collectiveness?
4. I have earlier done some good for others, knowingly or unknowingly. Can I recall and share those experiences with my group?
5. When my mind reaches a higher level of peace, what would I like to do?

9

MY BELOVED WILL ARRIVE TODAY* ...

The fear of death follows the fear of life. A man who lives fully is prepared to die any time.

- Mark Twain

There are quite a few things that we don't know about. There are also things we will never be told about in advance. The 'moment of transfer' is one such thing. Philosophers and spiritual *gurus* have advised us to live as if today is the last day of life. They have also told us that 'death' is not a matter of fear and that it rather deserves to be comprehended as a normal and natural phenomenon.

Death and the fear the thoughts of death can create in our mind have been conveniently used for manipulation for ages. The person who fears death becomes weak and

---

* Adopted from the lyrics of a Sufi bhajan Aaj mere piya ghar aayenge. This is not an exact transliteration. For a more precise understanding, discuss this in your Significance Group meetings.

then it is much easier to manipulate and control him and get him to do anything. This 'secret' has been exploited by fundamentalists and corporations providing certain services, and dictators at various points of time in the history.

Death is certain for all and can happen any time. This realisation changes something in our consciousness. People who have touched death and returned are inclined to use their bonus time for something significant *only*.

If you have come across such people in your neighbourhood, community or among your relatives, do share your observations with your group.

And do arrange a workshop based on the book *The Choice* by Og Mandino with the help of your Significance Group leader.

When we are contented, happy and ever-ready for the moment, when we have done only good for the self and others, progress is a 'done deal', it is a certainty.

Each day is one day closer to that day! And till then be absolutely happy and stay focussed on making your own bit of contribution.

Searching within…

1. Have I ever heard someone talking about death with courage, completeness and integrity? When? In what context? With what flavour (helplessness / anxiety / fear / wisdom / anxiousness / courage or yet another emotion)?
2. What are the changes taking place inside me after accepting this truth?
3. Victory is when fear crumbles down completely. If I am feeling scared, is it fair to suppress it, negate it, or get suppressed by it?
4. If I am feeling scared, who and what can help me?
5. Write a small note on: *My next day / next week / next 60 days.*

10

FORGIVE EACH OTHER AND ACCEPT EACH ONE. THIS IS NOT A FAVOUR TO OTHERS BUT A FAVOUR TO THE SELF

"*The good life is one inspired by love and guided by knowledge.*

- Bertrand Russell

An episode in the life of Buddha goes like this. The rule for becoming a disciple of Buddha was simple: forgive and accept everyone. Buddha used to say, "Forgive all who have ever troubled or tortured you, then come and sit in my *satsang*." A person once came to him and said, "I can forgive everyone but two persons in my life. Please show grace..."

Buddha looked at him compassionately and said, "Fine, some concession for you. Forgive and accept only these two and come here for *deeksha*."

Accidents hurt the body, some incidents hurt the mind. We treat the injury on the body quickly. However (almost cautiously), we preserve the injuries on the mind. This is strange as well as unfortunate.

Keeping the mind light and clean is a great favour to oneself. This is only (and completely) in our own control. Forgiveness is the first step towards this.

Forgiveness has three dimensions: forgiving the self, forgiving others, and asking for forgiveness from others.

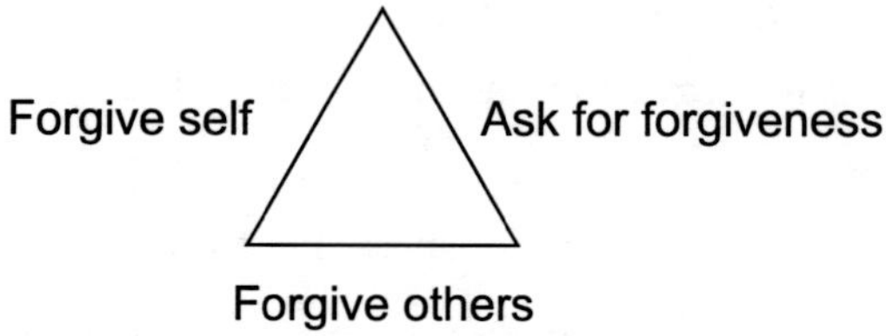

Not forgiving the self is just as painful and hurting as not forgiving others. We waste many years carrying guilt for something that happened when we were still not as mature, when we could not control our outbursts, and when the other factors were not in our hands, and so we missed achieving certain goals.

The mind becomes light when we forgive others and our own self. Recall the traits of the mind? It tends to stay stuck on something. Once it stays stuck in one place, it is then difficult to move it from there.

If the mind gets stuck at the guilt or blame, it just cannot feel fine. It then, loses on its power and positive traits. How? Emotions such as complaints, indignation, enmity, envy, hate, malice, aversion, hostility, and guilt are like weights tied to our legs. Try running with a stone tied to your leg. When we are getting ready for a long haul, we need to get rid of these weights; we need to drop them completely.

It is quite possible that with time going by, others have forgotten the incident that caused us so much anger and hate; but we are still stuck

After forgiving others, we must *accept* them unconditionally as they are.

Forgive and accept others for our own good. It is said that we start attracting the qualities of the person whom we constantly think about. These qualities start leaving impressions on our consciousness due to repetitive thinking.

In the context of the principles of *karma* and nature, 'bad' people (or the ones we consider 'bad') give us an opportunity to become good by becoming *'bad'* (so to say) themselves. It is often said greet the 'bad' person first, then the others.

Forgiving is, and should always be, an internal process; there is no need to explicitly express this gesture. There are two reasons for it. First and foremost, it is for one's own sake, as discussed in the previous paragraphs. Secondly, some people will not know how to handle themselves after being forgiven. (After being forgiven, ideally one should become cordial.) They may feel and express superiority or elation of some kind as if you have stooped down. This kind of behaviour is a personality complex. Be careful about it, without letting the other person know. This strange behaviour (that arises from the space of his ignorance) should not cause you a hurt again.

After we accomplish the three aspects of forgiving (forgiving others, forgiving the self, and asking for forgiveness), then comes the need to add the fourth dimension.

I call it 'community forgiving'. This is required, especially now, because in the name of protecting the community, we have collectively behaved like individuals: treating one another with intolerance and malice.

We must come forward in small groups and exercise the three tenets discussed earlier. The community must accept its collective bad behaviour and forgive itself. Communities must seek each other's forgiveness. Communities must forgive each other.

This can be one of the milestones in re-establishing harmony within human society and across man-made boundaries that we call 'nations'. Maintaining an environment where nations continue to have a rift could be due to the malice of a few who intend to enjoy supremacy or sell arms. With the course of time and events, such duplicity does get exposed.

Forget nations and humanity. Forgiving has a social and financial implication too. And in more than one way. When in disgust, we lose our own efficiency. There is so much that two co-workers, neighbours or brothers can accomplish if they forgive each other and come together. But what is happening? Just the opposite! Instead of harbouring oneness that could result in peace, prosperity and respect for organisation, society and family, we have disagreements, lifelong conflicts and wrangle. In addition to dealing with hard-core crime, courts are also busy addressing cases arising from these fermenting emotions. It would be wise to stay stuck in a row only if it is beneficial (a possibility which is rare and too expensive). Non-forgiveness only results in waste of time and inefficiency.

In fact, the world and time are moving so fast that forgiving alone may not be enough: we will have to be **light-hearted** (so that we learn fast, find our failures fast, and accomplish fast) and **friendly** (caring and reachable).

By the way, the experience one has after totally forgiving is quite profound and absolutely personal. Someone has said it aptly: *Only the strong can forgive*.

Nelson Mandela said about forgiveness at the time of his release after nearly three decades of imprisonment: "If I walked out of the door that would lead to my freedom; if I didn't leave my bitterness and hatred behind, I would still be in prison."

He had also said, "Forgiveness removes fear and liberates the soul". Mandela was the personification of forgiveness, really.

Forgiveness and mutual acceptance go together. What restricts our ability to forgive, or to accept others is, our tendency to form opinion: bad or good, about them

To get rid of using terms 'bad' or good' for people, we can think of them as 'young souls' and 'advanced souls' as Dr. Michael Newton has explained in his book *Journey of Souls*. 'Young souls' are driven by elements towards physicality (pleasure, attachment and desire only for worldly things) and ignorance of some kind. 'Advanced souls', on the other hand, may enjoy and use all the worldly comforts, but are oriented for self-actualisation and count on their intuitiveness.

Having this approach to think about people, what you will also notice that most of us swing and fluctuate between being 'young' and 'advanced' soul.

Searching within…

1. Whose thoughts hurt me the most? Has the incident, the impact and guilt not faded away?
2. One must not pretend to have forgiven. How can I forgive someone honestly, earnestly and completely?
3. Have I never ever hurt anyone? How can I seek his forgiveness cordially?
4. How do I feel after forgiving? Has the weight lifted from my mind?
5. If I had not gotten rid of this weight and dirt, I would have lost speed and wasted my time, isn't it so?
6. Make suggestions: How can we engage in seeking and spreading forgiveness without losing self-esteem or hurting that of others?

11

BEGIN PREPARATION FOR THE NEXT INNINGS TODAY

> *To be idle is a short road to death and to be diligent is a way of life; foolish people are idle, wise people are diligent.*
>
> **- Buddha**

It is almost guaranteed that life in the next episode will be much better than it is now. Why? Because we have intentionally caused harm to no one. It is another matter that because of ignorance we may not have done good to others. So, in effect, ours is a neutral, zero-balance case. We did not hurt others, nor did we do any good for them as such. [*]

To become useful for the self and others, we need to expand our comprehension or common-sense. What is 'common sense'?

Common sense arises when these five qualities blend with experience (1) Deep **understanding** of conversations,

---

* Please treat this as loving encouragement to explore further with confidence, not as a *guarantee*. The quality of life primarily depends on a number of other factors as you will note while reading this book and many other books. Three such factors are (i) the extent to which ego is mellowed down (ii) the *karma* accumulated and (iii) knowledge gathered during this lifetime.

behaviour and incidents (2) **Judgement** of what is fair and what is not (3) **Anticipation:** being able to see the impact of what happens today on the scenario of tomorrow (4) **Intuition**: ability to forecast what is likely to happen from subtle or negligible signals, and (5) Combining these four elements with the **courage** to take **small decisions**, decisions that give direction to our progress. These five elements plus experience is common sense.

Do have a discussion on this in your Significance Group.

What has this got to do with 'preparation'? What we referred to here as 'common sense', ancient and modern literature (that one may find inscrutable) calls *wisdom*. Wisdom is the theoretical knowledge that gets distilled through real-life experience, thus becoming useful for others as well.

The wisdom that comes through experience becomes an integral part of our own consciousness, our soul. We can consider this as if we are 'programming our DNA'. You may have noticed that the children of the next generation are slightly sharper than those from the previous generation.

I need to learn something - this thought might disturb us with next question that usually follows closely - *what do I need to learn?* It is easy to overcome this confusion by keeping this thought process: '*there is something that I cannot yet understand*'. If we can let this small idea sink into our patterns of thinking, then each situation, each incident and each individual who crosses our life will start pouring a new insight and wisdom. And after some time, we will wonder how the reality is, so much far away and different from our old patterns of thinking and how much, how fast have we changed.

In addition to this, reading good books, listening to and participating in constructive discussions, and asking questions with the intent to learn will also help. Keep taking baby steps and leave the speed of progress to time.

It is important to understand the next point. Like nutrients strengthen our body, wisdom strengthens our consciousness. A strong conscience can withstand and handle the gap between two lives and benefit most from the guidance available during this gap. A weak consciousness will not be as participative in the play and interplay of energies during the 'gap' just as a weak sportsperson cannot make it through the rounds of a tournament. He gets knocked off and quickly returns to the pavilion.

Searching within…

1. What am I going to do to alter the patterns with which I think and spend time?
2. Who will be my learning partners?
3. Do I really have a longing for learning? Why?
4. After attending a few meetings with the Significance Group leader, discuss, reflect upon and write a few lines on this topic: *When learning became entertainment.*
5. Can I feel the freshness and courage within me after adopting new ways of thinking?

12

Lessons from the University of Life

Life is a long lesson in humility.

- James M. Barrie

There was a moment in a young doctor's[*] life when he was utterly confused. He was in the final years of his professional education and he had to decide which way to go. His newborn son suffered a one-in-a-million deformity in his blood vessels around the heart. The blood vessels that should carry purified blood to the body parts were doing just the reverse. In spite of being surrounded by the best medical facilities and brains, the infant survived only three weeks. Disheartened by this, the young doctor decided that he would not pursue a career in a medical practice dominated by chemicals and technology. He made up his mind to master therapies based on psychology.

It took doctor's career of around 25 years and a client to decode the meaning of this event. The client in a

---

* Please read the full story in *Many Lives, Many Masters* by Dr Brian Weiss.

super-conscious state uttered to the doctor that the short-lived child was, in fact, a very advanced soul and he had travelled to this planet only to indicate a path to young, confused doctor.

The University of Life imparts teaching in slow and subtle ways, using a well-timed course of events. It took (i) an infant, (ii) about 25 years of time, and (iii) a client for Dr Weiss to realise how events shape the life and help us learn a new perspective. For me to realise this, it took all these plus the following:

i. a few more years and series of experiences that turned Dr Brian Weiss to an author documenting his personal observations on multiplicity in life and the messages and purposes hidden inside life
ii. a copy of one of his book reaching the school library where my wife is a teacher
iii. my wife introducing the book to me (about two years ago), and
iv. for me to somehow read that book. (I say 'somehow' because the initial 35–40 pages of the book *Messages from the Masters* were not to my taste).

In the following pages I share how some of the insights from this book, coupled with my revised perception on my relationship with one of my sons, helped me become gentler and compassionate person.

The ripples of *karma* spread and work in incredibly

fascinating manner. We may fail to see the connections between the events because the events may be spaced far apart from each other in terms of time and place. However, there is a Big Plan in progress.

It may appear too complex. One soul had to be here and take the pains to escort the doctor through the confusion. Another soul had to meet him after 25 years to tell what the lesson was.

Here is the point: We can get stuck or move forward in life because of one of these three factors.

1. **Confusion**: when we are stuck and unable to decide; unable to see through
2. **Ignorance**: when we are blind to what we should know
3. **Appropriate lessons**: when we overcome the two and seek out or reach a decision

Now, the faster we see the connection between the events, the lesser the time we 'waste'. That can happen through reflections only. Let me share my case.

I have twin sons. One of them is easy to connect with, while connecting with the other was usually not so easy for me. And it was quite an obvious and accepted fact that for some unknown reason, we two (my son and I) did not connect. We went through several bouts of blaming, withdrawal, voice-raising, and anger for about twenty years. I was always able to, unfortunately, justify my stand,. After reading the young doctor's incident I projected the parallels upon my circumstances, reflected and realised that my son had come here to indicate that I still needed to learn to be compassionate. I did get the hint and quickly discovered *compassion* as an element of my being. *It was already there!* Without this realisation, I had been so hurtful. I never felt so humbled in my life.

The lessons that life has to offer are too subtle and absolutely non-academic. A few examples follow. To learn these lessons however, I urge you not to rely on self-help books or mentors alone, the learning must be absolutely personal, felt, profound and experiential, so much that our values, thoughts and behaviour undergo a permanent transition.

Here are examples of the lessons life has to offer:

- Patience
- Compassion
- Love, oneness
- Forgiveness and acceptance
- Sharing, charity, service
- Harming no one, by action, words or intentions
- Learning a skill to be useful to others
- Discipline and self-control
- Checking greed, desire and aversion
- Simplicity, spontaneity

- Courage
- Appreciation and preservation
- Capturing the joy of the moment, humour
- Decisiveness, firmness, action-orientation
- Speaking uplifting words and values alone

You may call these lessons, you may call these virtues. Let me reiterate; do not think that you *know* them all till you are able to see them working *for* you, and tangibly enhancing the quality of your life.

A few words on doubts and questions. Subtle lessons do not come packed in a prescribed syllabus - content, methodology, sequence. So, these few rules of thumb will help, especially if we are having a mentor to guide us.

1. Not every doubt and question can be answered through words. The mentor may know the answer or solution, but he may not be able to / may not want to explain it with words. Verbal explanations are sometimes inappropriate and maybe even counter-productive.
2. We should not expect all doubts and questions (with stress on 'all') to be cleared within one session.
3. Doubts and questions are the stepping stones for inner progress.

4. Helpful doubts and questions arise from reflection.
5. Unresolved doubts and questions should not result in enraged behaviour. We should let the time respond.
6. We need to learn to be at peace with having unresolved doubts and questions, yet seeking.

Religion is an ancient system to educate people. Though ancient, religion is a man-made system. The name of religion is almost like the name of the school that we know today. *(Which school does your son study in?)* Like schools of today, religion had been a tool to (i) organise people and then (ii) educate them. Depending on the need of the hour and the learner's appetite and capacity to learn (yes, just as we have different levels of capacity to eat or work, we do have different levels of capacity to acquire and assimilate knowledge) the religion as a system usually has three progressive aspects to it: rituals, stories and deep profound discourses (an ideal discourse covering lessons for the management of life or lessons from the phenomenon called life itself) for advanced learners.

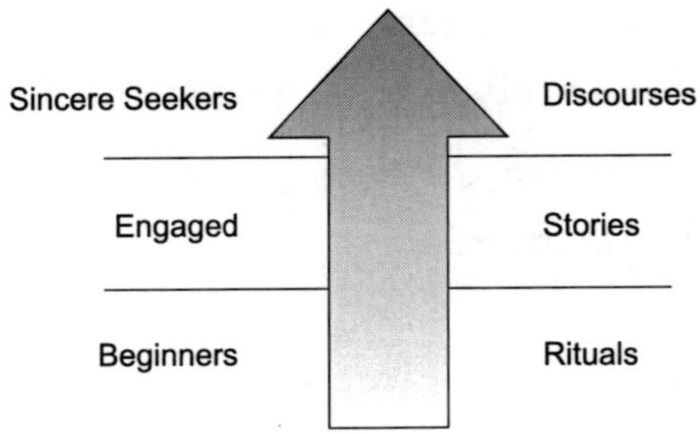

I am sure each religion, regardless of its time and origin, imparts the subtle lessons of the 'University of Life'.

Searching within…

1. Can realisation be a complete learning by itself? Why / why not?
2. Why do we miss our own shortcomings and blind spots?
3. Can I, in the next three days, see what indications people and situations have for me to learn?
4. What kills our sensitivity?
5. Are these lessons of life worth reviewing over and over again?
6. How much can one learn in one human life? Why can one get stuck?

13

It is not essential to understand it all

Only a life lived for others is a life worthwhile.

- Albert Einstein

When the mind opens up to the thought process that *I need to learn something*, we may face another anxiety: *I need to learn everything, understand everything.* 'Everything' is the root of many problems. There is no end in *everything*. Learning is like eating food; everyday, following a routine, with each of us having a different capacity to digest.

More than learning, it is rewarding to remain in the process of learning. We are accountable to taking good care of our consciousness. We must keep checking frequently to see if, by any chance, it is getting weakened. The symptoms of a weakened consciousness are: low energy, low courage, loss of purpose and purposefulness, anxiety, instability, disturbance, confusion, sadness, being disheartened, having no pertinent questions, having no quest.

The treatment for all these symptoms is not learning but staying in the learning process.

We understand nothing, understanding is given to us by the grace of the Infinite Wisdom.

It is the quality of our consciousness to be able to learn and preserve the new insights, not that of the cells of the brain.

What more do I explain or write? I do not know everything.

One of the tweets from Sri Sri Ravi Shankar reads thus: *Curiosity is the beginning of mind, wonder is its culmination.*

Searching within…

1. There is something that I need to learn and I have limited time and capacity to do that. Even on realising this, am I at peace with myself?
2. Consciousness is purified by knowledge, and purified consciousness can contain more knowledge, during this life and beyond. To be able to understand is the quality of consciousness. Am I able to tangibly feel this?
3. Can I see myself as my consciousness sees me?
4. How free is this consciousness – within me as well as beyond? Every time I sense its presence around or within, do I feel fresh, as if I just took a bath?
5. Does this consciousness talk to me? What does it say?

14

THE FASTER THE JOURNEY, THE MORE THE EXCITEMENT

> *One way to get the most out of life is to look upon it as an adventure.*
>
> **- William Feather**

Most of our journeys are cyclical: that is, we go somewhere and come back.

And most of the journeys are taken up with a specific purpose: entertainment, social courtesy, professional engagement or business.

When the purpose is accomplished, the mind feels hearty and we return happily to the place where we started. But if the purpose is not fulfilled, then we may have to take up another trip.

In the cyclical journey of our lives, there are four stages: life, death, the gap, and the embryonic stage back to life. The quality of the next life is better than the previous one in most cases. This is a general rule of nature and destiny unless we cause a major damage to someone. Most of us never do so.

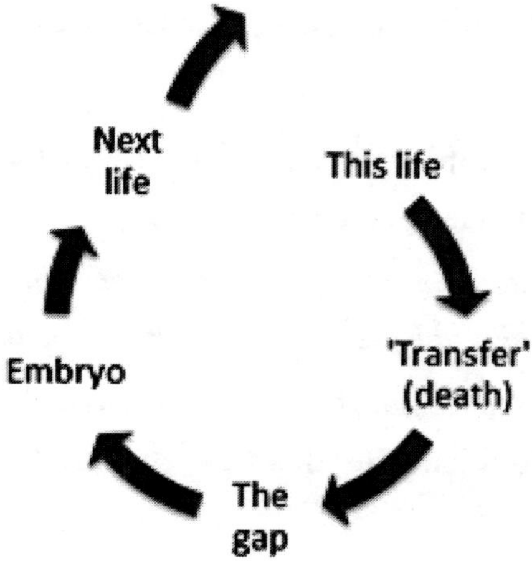

The journey in this life-cycle can be of four patterns (as we discussed in session 5).

- Each next life is better than the previous one.
- The next life is worse than this life, if we have caused pain or hurt to others with our intentions, thoughts, words and deeds.
- A pattern that is a mixture of the above two (one with many crisscrosses, ups and downs). We can sometimes be very good, sometimes very bad. We thus get stuck in the complicated web of our lives, not making any definite, qualitative progress.
- And the fourth: a total control on the decision regarding when one comes back in the physical form to the earthly life, the way all of us know it.

Two questions arise from this discussion:

1. Are we happy in this lifetime?
2. What is the level of control we have on this cycle of lives?

And it is not so difficult to find answers for these. Look back and analyse honestly and neutrally.

Has today / this week / this month been more significant than yesterday / the previous week / the previous month?

If yes, then feel sure that 'the vehicle' is making a forward progress. And the faster this vehicle moves, the more is the excitement.

If we are driving fast, we don't even notice the small trees, stones and potholes we cross. We take a note of all these only if we are moving slowly.

This applies to our life as well: pains, obstacles and constraints do come and go, but when we slow down, these appear too big.

There are three formulae for reducing troubles and increasing energy in life: action, action and action. This is not to be confused with positive attitude, it is all about positive action. The world is full of people with a positive attitude; we need people with a positive action.

Searching within...

1. What is more in my routine and thoughts: problems or actions?
2. After all, what is / are my problem / problems?
3. Is there no one in a more severe trouble than I am in?
4. How can I channelise my surplus time, energy, capacity and skills?
5. How will this make others' life a little better?

15

WHAT IS LEFT BEHIND, WHAT IS CARRIED ALONG?

> *Words are not trivial. They matter because they raise consciousness.*
>
> **- Richard Dawkins**

Life is an ongoing journey. Whose journey is it? What is that which is travelling?

It is wrong to think that the body is life. It is also wrong to think that breathing is life.

What is an embryo bestowed with first: breath or consciousness? The embryo has pulsation right from the first moment of its inception. The embryo begins to breathe much later.

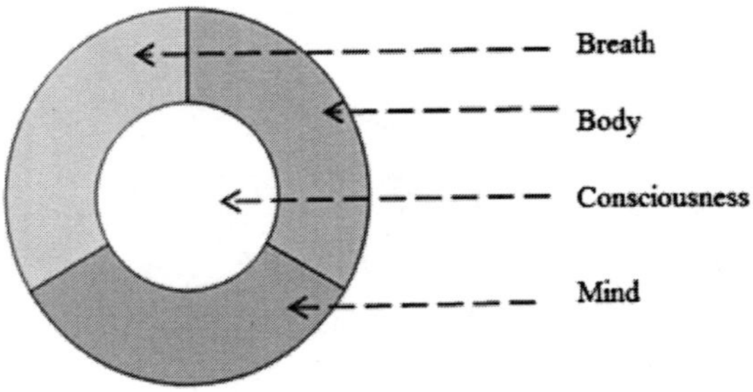

The air does not even enter the body that is in void of consciousness.

Also, it is wrong to assume that our accomplishments, our family, and our physical luxuries are life; neither the life is the profession or designation.

All these are present till we have a pulsation, a grain of consciousness, inside us.

Life is the consciousness. And it is this consciousness that travels.

The journey of our life *(who is this 'our' anyway?)* is the journey of consciousness.

Does the consciousness need any fuel, energy or nutrition to travel and expand, what does it need to move?

Nothing, it does not need anything additional. Pulsation and bounce are in its very nature – just do not burden it with unnecessary load. The way excessive luggage causes hassle in a journey, the consciousness loaded with negative impressions slows down.

Once the consciousness departs, what is left behind, what is carried along?

All that is physical in nature is left behind and all the impressions (*sanskaar*) are carried along as an integral part of consciousness.

What is retained are impressions. For example, after a two-hour movie, we remember very few scenes or dialogues.

Same is the case with our life. After living for many long years, there are but a few impressions of incidents and lessons that the consciousness retains. These impressions become or can become part of our personality in the next term of life.

So, what is retained? Just a few impressions!

To ensure we leave behind the right impressions on others and on our own consciousness, our focus should be exclusively on the way we think, our work and words. Our lifestyle, choices and behaviour must have a positive impact on others.

Though we have talked about the 'mind' as being a part of life, however, deeper analysis indicates that the mind is but a shadow of life. Till there is life, there is the mind. And like the small shadow at noon, when the sun is at its peak, when wisdom rises to full, the shadow of the mind becomes the smallest or dissolves completely.

It is of great value when each single word can reach out and leave impressions on the deeper intangible layers of our being and raise the level of consciousness. Engaging in this form of *karma* (speaking good uplifting words to the self and others) is easy.

Searching within...

1. Can I feel the pulsation, the subtleness, and the tenderness of my consciousness (the inner self)?
2. What are the things and who are the people that give me a feeling of bondage or pain? How can I surrender them all?
3. What should I do to establish a 'special' relationship with my consciousness?
4. The way I am living now, can it be called an 'active' life? How can I get to a state of total peace (at the level of consciousness) and action (at the level of the body)?
5. How can I maintain this unique balance always, time and again?

16

HAPPY DEPARTURES

> *The bond that links your true family is not one of blood, but of respect and joy in each other's life.*
>
> **- Richard Bach**

When our body is hurt, it pains; there is a close relationship between the feelings of pain and our connectedness.

At the moments of departure, everyone feels this pain, because at some higher level we are all are connected, we are all one.

However, if this pain is caused by ignorance (*thoughts that dying and death culminate in pain and torture*) then it is undesirable and inappropriate.

Around the moment of transfer, as reported by most of NDE cases, there is nothing like pain. If there is pain, it is the one caused by our own resistance to accept the process and the pain caused by the force one may emotionally exert to run away from the process. This resistance has its roots in unawareness and ignorance. Transfer is a complex and timeless system of transformation and purification of energies.

Will a drop of water feel pain by dissolving into the ocean? The drop also begins to flow after the merger.

All of us need to jump one day. The swimmer wins by swimming. However, he has to develop skills for diving as well as swimming.

Hence, keep the mind contented, at peace, and happy each and every moment. At the moment of taking a dive, it will help us as well as the others around us. Anxiety and pain ought to be minimal for all.

Departure and then returning – these are eternal truths; accepting this gives us strength and courage.

The pain caused by connectedness is valid. However, let it not turn to grief, heartache, helplessness or seizure. Feel the connectedness and the oneness, then pain will reduce quickly.

After the manuscript of this book had been written, it was going through review and editing. One morning, my son made an interesting observation. (By the way, I had never seriously mentioned to my sons the theme of what I had been writing because I felt they were too young with whom to discuss this topic). He said over phone, "I got short-listed through extempore speech rounds to join AIESEC. The topic was *if there was no death*." I got curious: both as father and as someone writing on this subject. I asked him what he spoke. As he gave some details, I could figure out he had made a fine speech with some very good points. For example, without death, the hall where he was speaking would have been much more crowded. The planet would not have sustained because death is the source of food for someone else. Everyone dies, be it man, animal or plants.

This observation was particularly striking. He had said that if there was no death, he would not have been 20, but 200, 500, or 1,000 years old. How profound! On transfer, we leave behind our age and get a new quota – our fresh quota of 60 or 70 or 80 years.

Life is a joy; the cycle of lives is also a joy.

Searching within…

1. What is my message to my dear ones in my absence?
2. What am I doing to stay contented, at peace and happy with others who matter?
3. Can I understand and appreciate the meaning and significance of the cycle of lives?
4. What are the two reasons of pain at 'that moment'?
5. At 'that moment' how does the mutual synergy change among the body, breath and consciousness?

INTERMISSION

> *The voice of the intellect is a soft one, but it does not rest until it has gained a hearing.*
>
> **- Sigmund Freud**

You are embarking upon an unusual but invaluable journey of self-discovery. If it has been overwhelming this far, take a break and come back.

17

PAINS OF THE BODY? LET THEM NOT BECOME PAINS OF THE MIND

Death is no more than passing from one room into another. But there's a difference for me, you know. Because in that other room I shall be able to see.

- Helen Keller

A body perfect in every sense – only rare people get it. On the other hand some of us are *expert* at finding flaws even in a perfect body. In few others a sense of vanity sets in about being beautiful or smart. By the way, for how many years does this 'perfection' sustain?

Little pain combined with large I-ness; this is enough for us to forget that there are so many others having 10, 20 or 50 times more pain or trouble than what we are going through.

It is a fact that the health and energy levels of the mind and the body move together. It is also true that just as the body affects the mind, the mind affects the body.

And the mind after all is a 'poor' mind. It will stay wherever we fixate it. However we keep it (happy or disturbed), it will so stay.

The mind is slightly notorious. It is not the logic (brain), it is not the consciousness, it is not our intellect, and it is not exactly our creativity also. Still our mind is ours and ours alone.

We ought to be careful about how our mind is handling us. Feeling happy at the level of the mind is the first requirement for us to stay happy and active.

What is this mind?

I honestly do not know what this mind is. However, there are hints that it has sufficient strength to either reduce or raise our energy level, and then the same energy runs the body.

And because activity is a sign of life, I am quite sure the mind is also in direct communication with the consciousness.

If there is a trouble in the body, be grateful that a few of the past *karma* are getting washed away. Be grateful that we are not one of those thousands, even millions, who have much severe, much complex ailments. And most of all, be grateful that these are the pains of the body (and will ultimately get 'treated'); not the pains of the mind, intellect, memory or consciousness. Think for a moment about the suffering people with such deformities are going through: they may not even be able to verbally express their pains.

This does not mean we disdain or ignore the body. Just do not let the pains of the body turn into pains of the mind.

Troubles in the body may, in fact, give us a reason to lead a life of significance and lead by setting a good example for others to follow.

ꕥ

Searching within…

1. What did I accomplish in spite of the pains and limitations of my body?
2. What are my thoughts about the flaws and pains in my body?
3. The mind can get weak due to the body or the body can get strength from the mind: what am I letting happen?
4. How can my body contribute to a significant life?
5. 'Life' is made of four components; the body is one of them. What are the other three?

18

Got something, lost something? Understand the principles of *karma*

> *As a well-spent day brings happy sleep, a life well spent brings happy death.*
>
> **- Leonardo da Vinci**

The principles of *karma* are very interesting and logical, they are also absolutely relevant today.

They are relevant because these principles explain in detail the cause-effect relationship. *If this, then that.* If one cooks, then one will get food. If one gets into an argument, then he will experience stress.

After birth, from the day we develop a sense of awareness, we desire something: the attention of parents, good scores in academics, a new car, a great job, or new gadgets.

We do work hard to accomplish these desires. However, the results are always not necessarily exactly the same as we expected. We lose something, we achieve something.

And the 'impressions' of success-failure keeps getting accumulated 'somewhere'. Repeated failure and loss lead to irate behaviour, anger and helplessness; repeated or easy success may lead to arrogance, vanity and a superiority complex. Both the extremes are some kind of 'dirt' on the mind-consciousness.

The principles of *karma* offer an explanation as to why our efforts do not yield in proportion to our efforts. (You may have by now had a discussion or workshop with your Significance Group leader on the book *Theory of Karma*). A fair understanding of these principles relieves us from the feelings of burnout and despair.

These principles are applicable on the other extreme as well; a scenario where results and comforts are received without much effort. It amounts to spending from the 'bank balance' of *karma*. An intelligent person, instead of getting elated by this, will turn humble, and engage in collecting more good *karma*. He will do so from space of awareness that feelings of arrogance and complacency (on receiving easy rewards) are the starting point for treating others improperly, and thus falling into *karmic* trap of cause-and-effect.

We commit *karma* in four ways: intentions, thoughts, words, and deeds. Although this is not a rule, it is quite possible that the sequence of the length of time required for yielding an outcome is just the reverse of this. Intentions may throw results after such a long time that fall beyond this lifetime. The simple illustration below will help you understand this.

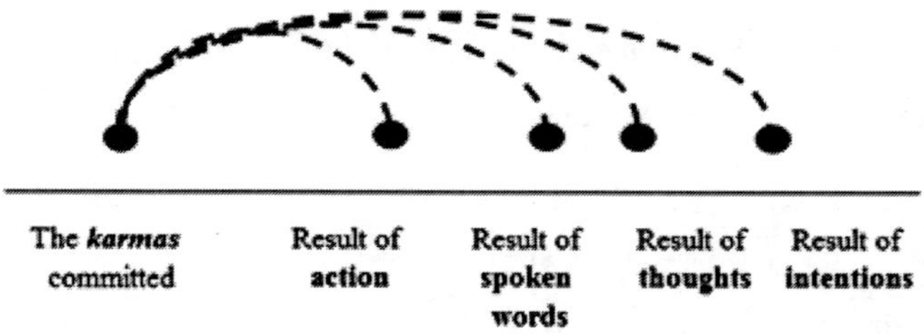

The 'intention' as *karma* deserves further illustration. A single idea combined with good intention can convert into service. When combined with bad intention, it can convert into crime. Take for example, buying or driving a car. When combined with the intention to serve others, it is good *karma*. But when combined with the intention of troubling someone, robbery or for simply flaunting, then it amounts to bad *karma*. This also applies to every profession or business. Business is a system that can 'absorb' the intentions of greed (*the need to make the most profit or wealth from a product or idea to become rich, richer or the richest)* or the intention of self-fulfillment (*we need to be a pioneer in this technology)* or the intention of serving society (*how can we make maximum people benefit from this technology or idea)*.

This is where the fourth principle of *karma** needs to be explored. The fourth principle is very simple, it is so simple that it does not require any explanation. *No good karma remains unrewarded, no ill karma remains unpunished.* In

* Cross reference: Discussion 5

fact, this law is so universal and so straightforward that we can we can use it for reverse analysis. *Karma* is *karma* by itself. If someone is feeling punished, we can call it the results of previous bad *karma* and if someone is feeling rewarded, we can call it the results of good *karma* from the past.

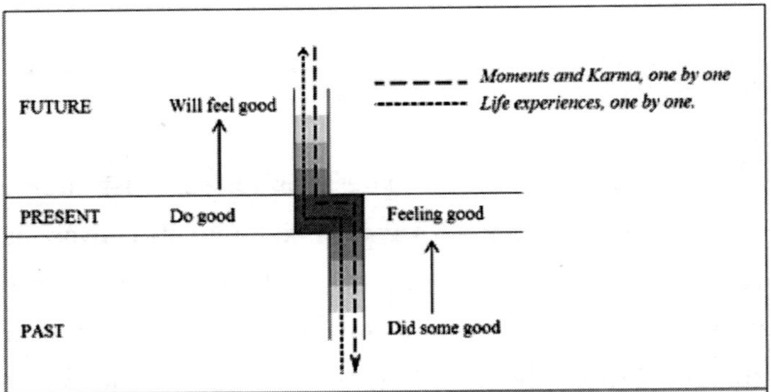

With passing time, Karma turns to become experience.

This illustration explains only the 'good side' of the process. *Did some good in the past, hence feeling good today.* However, the opposite is also true. We need to remember and recall this time and again.

This knowledge should give a new angle to look at factors and circumstances. All that we go through are *Karmic* in nature, and these are carefully aligned for our learning, not for punishment. Thoughts of punishment give rise to fear, and makes us run away from reviewing circumstances as learning opportunities.

(We may have a confused and overlapping awareness about what *karma,* punishment and learning are. To clarify myself, I looked up for origin of word 'discipline' because this word seemed to integrate the three. The word 'discipline' in its Latin original form meant 'instruction, knowledge'; which, with descend in time, got transitioned to 'mortification by scourging', or, in more simple words, suffering and embarrassment. How sad!)

For learning to occur, one must go through the factors and circumstances remaining constantly engaged in reflective dialogue with the self. Hence so many questions all along the sessions in this book. A well-formed question helps not only in learning, but also in remaining open to learn, in remaining engaged and joyful through the process. Without such questions, we may fall in trap of blaming (blaming destiny, blaming others, blaming situations) and develop feeling of irritation about the factors and circumstances, or even worse, develop a counterproductive question: *why me?*

Most of the times, most of us are too busy to think and realise what our intentions are. Asking multiple times this simple question – *what do I want* – helps. Usually, we want sensory pleasures or resources and instruments that can provide such pleasures. There is no harm in this but when we get stuck at this level, it can result in frustration after some time.

Yet another reason to analyse the intentions time and again has to do with its pregnant nature. Intention quickly gives birth to an emotion, a thought, or words. These three mix with each other and become our mindset and action, and when this stays long enough, it shows up as the pattern of behaviour. Behaviour is a pattern of action, a predictable one.

This is only a schematic explanation but this is how it may look if we could 'see' the correlations.

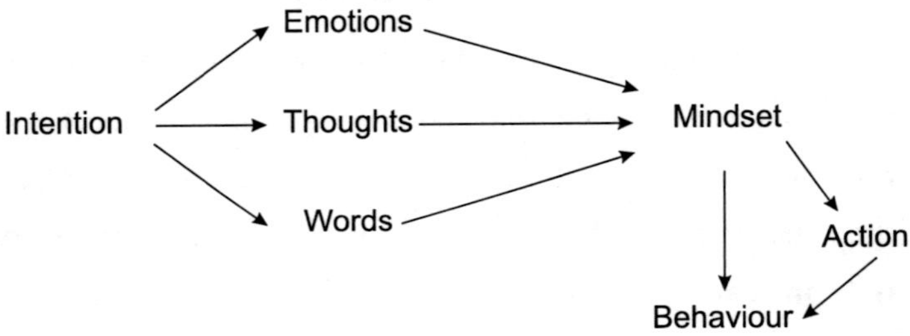

Understanding one's own intent saves time. Knowing *what I want* is the *sutra* for having focus. It is better said in Hindi: *Neeyat se bane niyati* (accumulated intentions make the destiny). On the other hand, being able to understand other's intent saves us from bluff and heartbreaks. In fact, being able to understand our own intent and those of others is THE secret sauce for working through the life with ease.

Karma management and money management are not too different. We need the luxury of some of it today and some of it in the future as well.

Karma and discussion about it remain incomplete till we explore what Free Will is. *Karma* is profound because it works in conjunction with free will, the freedom to choose between two or more options that we always have. Each and every moment in this life and beyond this life, the freedom to choose the intention, thought, words and action is never taken away from us. Even in the spirit world, they say, it is we who choose when to return to life on the Earth again, what kind of body to adopt, the family, the location and the life situations.

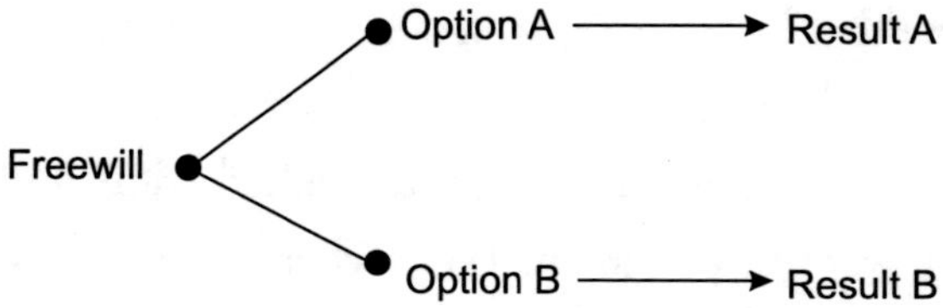

It is worth watching the self using this bliss of free-will. We choose sometimes conscientiously, sometimes ignorantly, between fear and courage, rest and work, being cynical and being appreciative, being hopeful and getting hopeless, harshness and gentleness, greed and delayed gratification, and so on.

Until the answer to this simple question *what do I want* becomes 'nothing', we are yet to operate from the space of true consciousness. Let me explain this. Suppose we go for a job, what do we want from it? The answer can be 'salary at the end of month'. Good. Here, the 'want' is 'salary'. Now hypothetically, if the salary is transferred into my account every month regardless of going to office or not, will I still continue in this job? Or, on the other extreme, if there is no salary at the end of the month, will I still go to office?

Salary or job is not the point in question. The real question is *what is that we will do regardless of the gratification or rewards attached to it, do it happily and whole-heartedly.* When we ask these questions and arrive at some clarity, then we start realising what our intentions are. The true action is the one that happens regardless of the thoughts of outcome or reward. It is said that true success and contentment comes when we do what we are naturally gifted with so well that people want to pay for it. (A teacher teaches so well that parents and students want to pay for it, because his teaching can help students understand the subject, pass the exam, and become a better person.)

Let us also understand the spoken words as *karma*. Spoken words are like instruments or tools. Whenever used, they will do their job of hurting or building others. Once spoken, the intentions become secondary. After saying insinuating, hurtful or demeaning words to others and then defending by saying "*it was not my intention to hurt you*" does not work. The words have already done their job. The *karma* has already been committed.

Gaining or losing are both on the right side of the *if-this-then-that* formula. We need to strengthen the left side, that's it! The 'if' part is called *karma* and that consumes some time. Time is another name for life.

The root of results is action. Action is rooted in words, words are rooted in thoughts, thoughts are rooted in intentions, and intentions are rooted in destiny. Destiny is product of accumulated *karma*. Unless sufficient good *karma* has been accumulated, right intentions will not even arise.

Dr Weiss writes that *we fear death so much that we miss on the very purpose of life*. When fear is present, plenty of energy and time get wasted. Once free from fear, one could think well and use the time to act; thereby staying immersed in living usefully.

Remaining idle and passive is losing time, and losing time is losing life. Shifting focus from '*what will I get*' to '*what has to be done / what needs to be done*' can get us busy. This will speed up our life and we will not even notice the pains and troubles we have.

Searching within…

1. Pause and take stock. What troubles / failures are causing distress to the mind? What successes are causing egotism?
2. Have I been able to understand the typology of *karma*? What types do I need to focus on?
3. Is it difficult to accept the principles of *karma*? List a few luxuries that we enjoy for which we have done nothing.
4. Can some of the *karma* give good results time and again?
5. Does it take more energy or work to engage in good *karma* compared to the energy or work required for ill *karma*?

19

Never before, never after due moment. Discuss death openly. Initially fear may rise, then it will disappear

> *Discussion is an exchange of knowledge, an argument an exchange of ignorance.*
>
> **Robert Quillen**

Is engaging in discussions about death likely to attract ill-fate? Will thinking about death bring it forward? Will it inflate fear? Can such a discussion be ominous?

Death is a certain and essential component of life-cycle; it is a halt for cooling the engine and cleaning the windshield. At least death will never arrive before time, this is guaranteed. Our small-minded thinking about it makes no difference; few plans are in the control of the Infinite Wisdom only. A passenger may think whatever he wants about the arrival time for a train he is waiting for. However, the train moves under the control of someone else, under a much bigger plan.

So for a brief period, talking openly about death with mature discussion partners is not harmful. It is rather helpful because this discussion will help sublimate the suppressed fear or aversion we have about death.

A pinch of fear is built in by the nature for our safety. However the rest of fear is imposed (by self or others), and this portion of fear is dysfunctional. We need to manage or shed this part of fear The people who are acclaimed to be brave and courageous, who have demonstrated deeds of exemplary boldness, they too, at some point of time, had their own fear and conquered it. Being aware of the fear we have is helpful to manage it; instead of being *aware about it*, some people get carried away by it.

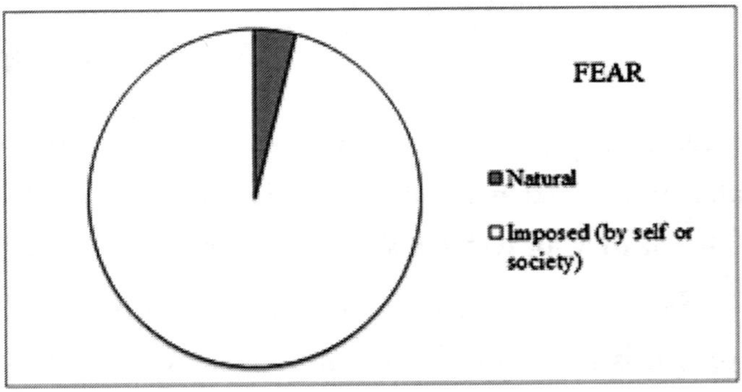

Once we have won over the fear of death with proper knowledge, other small fears (that of losing repute, losing assets, humiliation, etc.) get dwarfed. This is when the mind and the consciousness get soaked in peace. It even changes our outlook of life, people and incidents. When we overcome fear, we feel love and gentleness towards all and we see less of their faults (and our own); the unhelpful urge to always be perfect and control things reduces.

If this state of mind is combined with clarity about the principles of *karma*, life is bound to be active and significant. I firmly suggest that at least life partners and business partners (whose being together and working together matters to them as well as to few others) should have a dialogue in the right spirit, with the right words, and at the right time: what A does if B leaves first, what B does if A leaves first.

Understand the hypothesis of a 'significant life'. In the cyclical web of lives, we will go through many lives (being born again and again). Each of us is on our own individual journey. Now, take a look around. All the lives that we know can be broadly classified into four categories.

A. Life where struggle is more
B. Life of 'surviving' well – where everything is okay and fine.
C. Life that is full of success, wealth and happiness but all within the limited boundaries of the individual and family
D. Life that is significant: where something was done to facilitate others' happiness and progress for a much longer time-frame, yielding positive results time and again, having a much broader vision beyond 'I-me-mine'

A note of caution: This classification is not really hierarchical in nature, but typological. What does that mean? This clarification denotes that one does not necessarily move up from A (life of struggle) to B (life of survival) and so on. One is at any one position at a time: either A, B, C or D.

A person with lots of money may be 'struggling' and another person with little money may be doing much significant work leading a significant life.

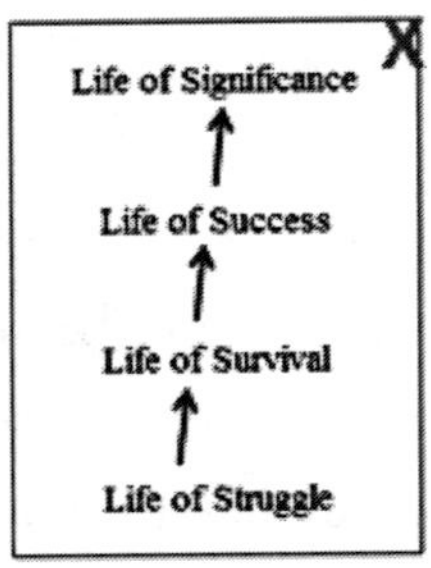

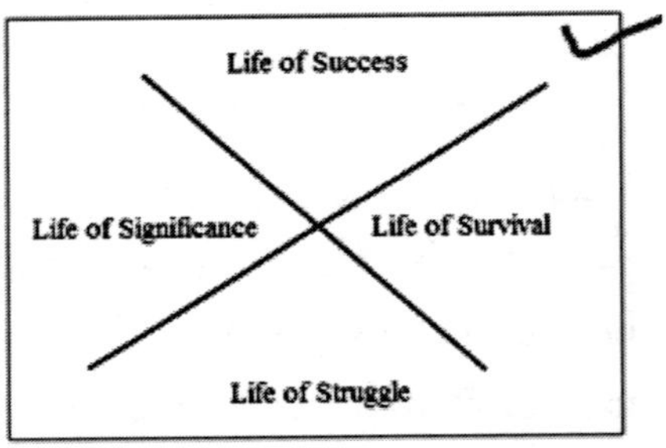

For a significant life, death is not an obstacle. To help others, they will return, using free will, again, whenever they decide to.

Searching within…

1. At what age do people usually start thinking (or are forced to think) about death?
2. Do people avoid or postpone thinking about death? If yes, why?
3. Do a quick *yes-no* survey with five people: *Do you want to lead a significant life?* And if they respond with a 'yes' then ask the next question: *Do you have a plan or strategy for this?*
4. Write your own reflections about the significant life.
5. What are the chances of your decisions being accurate and proper when they are taken under the influence of fear or pressure: low or high?
6. Do we have to win over fear again and again?

20

THAT IS NOT PAINFUL, PROVIDED THE PROCESS IS UNDERSTOOD

We ourselves can die with comfort and even with joy if we know that death is but a passport to blessedness, that this intellect, freed from all material chains, shall rise and shine.

- Mathew Simpson

What we call life has four constituents:

- **Body**, so that we can act on our thoughts
- **Breath**: This is the maintenance mechanism, essential for physical and emotional purification, repairs and biological processes.
- **Consciousness**: The basic pulsation, the source of energy
- The **emotional component**: Desire-detest, inclination, priorities, feelings, whims and imagination

The collective quality of these four components determines the quality of life.

Around the time of death, which I now prefer to call 'transfer', these four components undergo different changes. The previous statement is a simplified one. We can break it down to smaller pieces for further discussion.

Various parts and organs of the body begin to 'cool down' many hours prior to the transfer. But this does not cause pain.

The breath starts to become shallow. This also does not cause pain.

The consciousness can lift up from the physical level and see the entire process with the pair of eyes of an observer. This also does not cause any pain. In fact, based on the experiences shared by people who almost touched death and returned, we can conclusively say that with expansion and lifting up, it experiences unending gentle love and peace, wonder and welcome. Hundreds of interviews, videos of people who have had near-death experience, and research on NDE and trans-death experiences are now available. (See Appendix 1 also). Most of them describe it as consciousness meeting an eternal light and love, a cordial welcome, and some kind of spiritual feeling. Some of them even mention that it is during this expansion that they were subtly reminded about the 'agreement' (agreement about the 'why' – the purpose for which they had gotten this life).

Emotions get perturbed, resulting in a kind of chaos for the person who is being transferred and for the others around him. This can be painful if everyone is not sufficiently oriented, directed and aware of the process, and trained to handle this. The pain can aggravate if, out of ignorance, one deals with the process by forcing resistance and rigidity.

I have stressed throughout this book many times to keep the mind absolutely contented and at peace. The transfer is not all that painful. Imagine this: dozens of *people* are waiting for you, and when you arrive, they receive you with a very warm welcome saying, "*We love you.*" How can this be painful?

Searching within…

1. Just as the internet established new principles for business, communication and governance, a deep and precise understanding about 'transfer' is opening new dimensions for humanity and society. Have I collected a few reliable insights into it?
2. Do I remember the purpose of being given this life?
3. It is quite possible that in the near future, a community will form and treat 'transfer' as one of the 'learning experiences' of this life. The community will discuss and deliberate upon it. Would I like to be connected with such a community?
4. If the life was lived for accomplishing a positive and clear purpose, will there be emotional pain at the moment of transfer?
5. What additional thoughts and suggestions do I have to stay calm during the moment of transfer?

21

Staying happy is easy. Do something for others with action, words, thoughts and intentions

Be happy. It's one way of being wise.

- Sidonie Gabrielle Colette

We may think leading a 'significant life' may be too demanding, that it may call for hard work or sacrifices, or it may diminish the charm and *chill* of life that we are currently enjoying.

It is logically true that the more the resources we have, the more we can do for others. Two kinds of resources, financial and intellectual, bring us to a position from where we can truly reach out to a very large section of society.

However, as we understood from the principles of *karma*, if there is 'I-me-mine' at the level of intentions, *karma* results in hardened ego. The irony is this: it is the ego that helps us begin some work. This work helps us gather all the resources required. It is quite an art – an art worth mastering; to keep working and surrendering (getting rid of) the ego.

Does that mean people with less financial and intellectual resources cannot do anything for others? There is a resource of the third kind: desire.

History is replete with hundreds of examples such as Nelson Mandela, Mother Teresa, Martin Luther King and Mohandas Gandhi who made a humble beginning. They took baby steps and ultimately touched the lives of millions of people, of entire nation.

So, do we have to become a 'great soul', a sage like them, and make sacrifices to lead the life of significance?

It is not so. Let us turn back to the principles of *karma* and understand them. To keep thinking only about the self is the root cause of all pain and feverishness. The act of helping others can begin with intentions. We can alter our intentions at every instance. For example, while paying the taxi fare, we can replace the thought that we are paying for *my convenience* with the thought that *this money can be used for the education of the driver's son*. This small change is sufficient to make a beginning, and this is not as difficult as we may have thought.

There is yet another aspect about helping others. Helping the self should precede helping the others. This implies emptying the mind and the heart. Unless this is done and because the mind is very smart, it senses quickly the duality if we are in pain ourselves and are trying to be good to others. It is not erroneous if such a thought sparks: *I am myself in trouble, how can I do good to others*?

How to empty the mind? Forgive and accept yourself, your past, and your circumstances. Whatever pain, guilt, remorse, and complaints there are, pull them out one at a time (these may be suppressed at much deeper levels somewhere). One may need to follow this two-step process: a) to bring them to surface (courage and guidance may be needed at this stage); then, b) to drop them slowly using prayer, writing, meditation, or discussion. Surrender them all, one by one.

We need to work with momentum to reduce 'emotional violence' to the self and others; all the other crimes and pains will disappear. Understanding and applying this thought requires courage. At least one select part of our society can take this initiative, and we can hope that the weak of today will follow the suit as they too gain access to the strength.

Only a clear, emptied, and burden-free mind can think and feel *for* others. First, do this good to yourself. In this form of service to the self, there is no greed.

There are two facets of doing good: a) doing good for others and b) doing good for the surroundings and the ecosystem in which we all live. Appendix 2 has many examples that will draw the point home as to how easy and possible it is to do something out of the 'I-me-mine' circle.

Remember this. Leading a 'successful life' has been in fashion for the last 5–7 decades. It has been an off-shoot of modern education and industrialisation. In the decades to come, leading a life of significance will be the trend.

(I have only one request to make. Keep all the good work away from corporate intervention because ideally such works and projects should not become a platform for branding and promotion for large companies.)

Sometimes our mind may trick us: *Why should I bother about others, who cares for me? I need to instantly see the outcome of what I do.* These thoughts need to be placed correctly. Someone somewhere thought that you would need good roads, good education, a good house, a handsome salary, and good food. Either we don't even notice it or we forget. *Karma* is really very strange. While creating these facilities, they may have had their own 'I-me-mine' facets, but we got our share of convenience, right?

ꕥ

Searching within…

1. What realisation sunk in after this discussion?
2. Prepare a list of people because of whose work we have all comforts. We are what we are and we are doing what we are capable of.
3. How easy or difficult is it to do good to others with words, thoughts and intentions? Why?
4. Take stock of the state of your mind after doing good to someone.
5. Experiment this. Bring out all the problems, complaints, bitterness, remorse or ego overclouding the mind, one at a time, on a piece of paper. Throw the paper into the dustbin. Repeat this exercise till the whirling ceases. (If you do this exercise 2–3 times a week, it may take 1–2 months or more for the mind to empty.) After this experiment, share your experiences with others.

22

At some level, everything will appear childish

> *To improve is to change; to be perfect is to change often.*
>
> **- Winston Churchill**

Have you ever seen photos of your childhood? Loose-fitting clothes, hilarious facial expressions, toys and friends. As time passes, all these appear too childish, don't they?

Every 7–10 years, we transform at the levels of body, mind, personality, outlook and values that direct our life. Whatever we are holding firm today will appear childish later.

Get the mind to this level of maturity; you will feel a great sense of peace and composure. You will actually realise that time is running fast, it is we who get stuck somewhere.

Continuous change is the law of life and nature. The gyre of time and that of life are not different. Still the mind and watch patiently the harmony of the two gyres and the patterns this harmony is creating. These patterns have a rhythm, a message.

Searching within…

1. When I watch all around with a still mind, can I hear a melody somewhere out there?
2. With softly shut eyes, can I see the movie of the story of my life so far (and that of time to come as well)?
3. What have been the three turning points in my life?
4. Do I feel that all this is like a drama?
5. Am I still left with something to complain about that I need to drop / surrender?

23

THEY ARE GOING TO FORGET!

"... in the school of the spirit, man learns wisdom through humility, knowledge by forgetting, how to speak by silence, how to live by dying."

- Johannes Tauler

Millions use the internet every day but how many remember Tim Berners-Lee?

Billions use the electric bulb but how many remember Thomas Edison?

Who remembers Henry Ford while driving a car?

We use cellphones; do we even know who Martin Cooper is?

All the pioneering work one does, whatever contribution, big or small, that one makes, it is going to be forgotten. In a way, it is good; otherwise all the time will get consumed in recalling them and being grateful to those who have made our lives so easy. Thus, having no time, we will miss the chance to do good to others.

People are going to forget, so should we not engage in significant tasks? There is a slight confusion in doing something significant. We get the feeling that we are doing good for others, whereas in the long run, it is we who are going to benefit. In fact, there is an 'I' in 'I will get benefitted'. And even a single thought of this kind (*I-ness*) can take away the spirit of work.

Engaging in significance is like sowing a seed. Sow the seed, take care of it, but think not about outcome: *who will enjoy the fruits and shadow?* Let others enjoy the fruits and the shade, and let them also forget you (the creator).

Creator, the Almighty, is used to being forgotten. His greatness lies in this quality.

By the way, what are you and I doing?

Others are going to forget our work, they are going to forget us. By forgetting, they free us. Memory is a kind of bond at one level, as well as a kind of bondage at another. It is good to be forgotten. Let us understand what this really signifies in the following paragraphs. Having this clarity is critical because **memories** and **emotions** are quite closely linked with each other.

We bind with others who have resembling or complementing emotional wavelength. Thus, matching the frequency, we develop what amounts to be a 'bond' – the oneness and cohesiveness we feel *with* and *for* each other. However, with the course of time, if only one of the participants grows (emotionally, professionally, socially or so), the same bond becomes a 'bondage'. At this point, the two of them should either re-synchronise or one must move up, because bondage is painful. It is, in fact, painful for both. Bond to bondage is a play and an interplay of emotions.

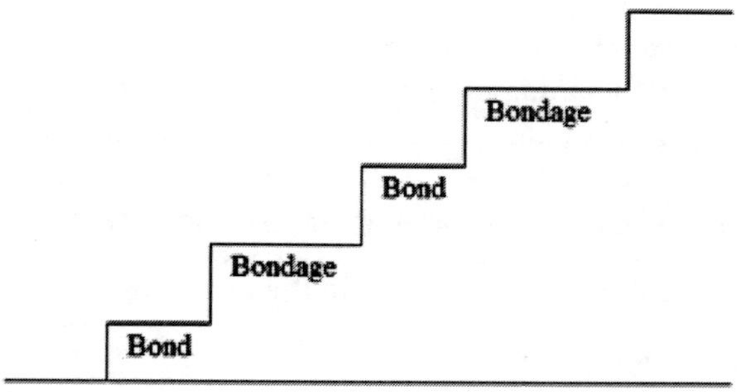

Moving up emotionally from bond to bondages, to higher bonds and higher bondages, when we are ultimately free of emotions, we are free of bonds and bondages. ***We are finally free***. Learning *how to accomplish this freedom* is one of the purposes of life, the utility of this one life.

Is our memory a little strange? We forget big things and we hold on tight to petty issues.

Searching within...

1. What is your opinion about being grateful?
2. How can we accelerate the act of doing good to one another?
3. When the mind is liberated, one needs a little music. Do you feel you need some music?
4. It seems that doing good to others is in our basic nature because doing so makes us feel complete. Do you also agree with this?
5. If people forget the good that we did to them, what should be our response or reaction?

24

A task that could not be completed or one that failed... The root cause? Ignorance or ego. Seek the real wisdom, it will cure ignorance as well as ego

> *Be ashamed to die until you have won some victory for humanity.*
>
> **- Horace Mann**

One of the most common reasons for regret or the 'alas moment' at any juncture in life arises from the tasks and projects that could not be completed or the ones that failed.

Five elements are required to work in conjunction with each other to conclude a project as desired (in time, successfully): desire, resources, efforts, acumen, and someone's good wishes / blessings.

1. Desire will arise and will be strong, if there is some accumulated *karma* from the past. Desires are the starting point for all tasks and projects. On the

positive side, desires make us active. However, too much of it can make us feverish.

2. The course of events (which is only partially in our control), will gather resources.
3. Efforts will come by when there is sufficient enthusiasm and high morale.
4. When personal experience combines with theoretical (heard, read or observed) knowledge, it becomes acumen.
5. And submission begets us the blessings and good wishes from others.

Ego is the biggest obstacle for all these. If 'I-me-mine' is attached to the *karma*, it bears no fruits of the quality that should culminate in rise of desires of the right kind.

Ego disturbs our harmony with time; it makes us want everything to happen as *we* have planned it (mostly 'now'. We get feverish about it. This disturbs the much-needed sync between time and events.

When ego (the identity) mixes with efforts - *I am doing this* - the person gets tired fast. If the 'I' is working, the 'I' will get tired. Getting free from the 'I-ness' increases our energy because then we know it is not the *'I'* at work.

An egotist feels that what he knows is all that there is. This blunts his acumen and he does not take accurate decisions. (Ego becomes the barrier between the good decisions that he could have taken and two other elements – intellect and intuitive apparatus – which we will discuss later in session 31).

An egotist also cannot submit himself to others. What he misses is others' good wishes and blessings – the elements that have the power of recommendation.

Seek the right wisdom, this will cure ignorance as well as ego.

What is right wisdom? This question may be quite puzzling. How can I be sure that this wisdom or the source of wisdom is right?

Do not resort to any short-cuts for finding the answers to these questions. Check yourself by reflecting and pondering, and then reach a conclusion. This process in itself is a unique experience.

How will I know if I am on the right track? You will feel yourself intimately close to Infinite Wisdom, your creativity will thrive, your desperation and distraught will fade away, and a grace will develop in your conversations, thoughts and personality.

How much time will it take to reach this level of connection with your inner guiding element? No one can guess for each other. You remember it right; scientists and philosophers have said that life has only two purposes: to progress on the path of seeking wisdom and to make contributions in service of the creation in accordance with one's own capacity.

Searching within…

1. Without interrupting or being suggestive, seek opinion with one senior and one junior person about the relation between success, efforts, ego, wisdom and acumen.
2. Conduct this '*yes-no*' survey with five people: Has/have any of your project/s been incomplete or unsuccessful? If yes, then what could be the reasons for that?
3. Think and then write or discuss: How does this world work?
4. What could be the difference between ego, self, vanity and pride?
5. Which is that one work you would like to complete? After this discussion, what will be your strategy?

25

THE BODY WILL DIE ONE DAY. LET NOT THE SPIRIT DIE TIME AND AGAIN, MANY TIMES

"Life is pleasant. Death is peaceful. It's the transition that's troublesome.

- Isaac Asimov

Let us return to the topic of death. One good thing about life and death is this (at least within the limited scope of our memory): both occur only once.

Thoughts about death usually slant towards two key concerns: the body will undergo a shutdown and the balance among the circumstantial factors will be disturbed.

Let us discuss a few details about both.

The body stops working, it becomes inert. Whenever something gets inert, we call it 'dead'. For instance, *the phone is dead* is quite a known expression. What do we call it if our good senses cease to work? How many times have we heard this 'I do not feel like…' from our own self and others? The body dies once. The spirit and good sense can die many times. Is that not a wonder?

Should the good sense die many times? All that we do or don't do begins at this sense. *I feel like taking rest today. I feel like going to the mall. I do not feel like going for bath now. I do not feel like attending the class…*

The mind and the good sense we have is very much part of our life. It's like driver software, isn't it? Do take good care of this component of life too!

What about the balance among circumstantial factors? Have you read *Who Moved My Cheese* by Dr Spencer Johnson? The surroundings and factors that we hold onto, that we depend upon, are all changing. Change is happening whether we like it or not, slowly or fast. The only way to spare oneself from a jolt is to be aware of this fact, accept it, and align oneself with this progression.

Change is another name for time. With time, our age, the way we walk, our orientation, our values, our preferences and every other factor and person around us mature, transform, transition, alter, modify, revamp and revise.

Change occurs so that one story ends and another begins. And somewhere deep down, we all are children and we learn through stories only, we learn from change.

Growth is in progressive imbalance. Observe this some time: when we are climbing a staircase or walking, we are mostly on progressive imbalance, i.e. on one leg.

Imbalance is momentary because nature brings back the balance. Nature loves newness and freshness.

Imbalance is momentary, pain is momentary. Life also is momentary. Keep the mind at peace. An unquiet mind experiences more pain.

MY elder brother made a beautiful comment while we were discussing this book project once. He said that most of the times, most of us are in a state of fight with our own life, having complaints, having stress and pain, having laidback stances, having grudges, having anger with life, having a fear of the future, and blaming life for this or that. It seems as though we are on one side and life is on the other side. The moment both come to the same side, the scene will change immediately.

By the way, what are we fighting with? We are fighting with something in which we are. It is like a fish fighting with water. Is life inside us or are we inside life?

What we call life comes from outside us. All energy (literally every form of *physical* energy) comes directly or indirectly from the sun and other planetary bodies. The *biological* energy comes from the air that we breathe; the air is present around us, almost timelessly. The water and food (all come from Mother Earth) and even the *psychological* energy come from experiences and lessons that shape our mindset; values and our persona originate from the society outside us.

Just as it happens in chemistry where we get a new compound by combining two or three materials; when the three forms of energy mentioned in the previous paragraph combine, we get a new form of energy called life.

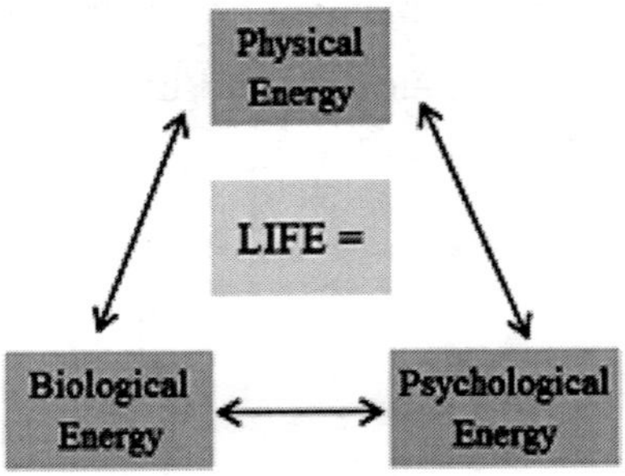

The moment we think of the word 'life', we think of it in terms of time: *the time available with us*. We need to look at life in terms of energy. Life is the force; it is the energy that is making us go around. It is *the* energy that can treat and cure many physical symptoms, most of the emotional symptoms, and almost every situational symptom that we are struggling with.

We need to give a chance to the energy called life. The life we have individually and the life we have collectively.

It is said that *zindagi zindadili ka naam hai,* i. e. life is where the spirit is high.

Searching within…

1. Why do I detest remaining passive?
2. Where is the control of mind?
3. Recall one episode of imbalance that ultimately recovered for better. Share the experience in your group.
4. Does our mind control us? Sometimes yes, sometimes no. What is your opinion?
5. Review the story of the life of someone who has passed away – an ancestor, relative or neighbour. What lesson do we get from his story?

26

IN PLACE OF FEELING SAD OR HAPPY, KEEP THE SPIRIT OF WONDER, EXPERIMENT, ADVENTURE AND COURAGE ALIVE

> *Some people are so afraid do die that they never begin to live.*
>
> **- Henry Van Dyke**

It is an old adage. *It is all a play of the mind.* In one of the earlier sessions, we discussed what happens to the body, breath, consciousness and emotions at the moment of transfer.

You will be able to recall this. During childhood, we went to Meena Bazaar and watched the giant wheel. Sitting on the giant wheel was an exhilarating experience, an experience of a different kind altogether, something where the three states of mind worked in conjunction: 1) **wonder** superseded fear 2) spirit of **experimentation** superseded anxiety (*let us sit on that once!)* and 3) **courage**.

And the combined effect of the three was something between joy and tension.

We experience a variety of emotions during our lifetime – joy, trouble, attachment, zeal, affinity, hatred, rejection, aversion, acceptance, mania and vanity. All these are either positive or negative.

However, there is an 'eternal joy' which is neither positive, nor negative. It simply ***is*** (eternal, timeless, calm, massive, and flowing within itself).

We may experience this eternal joy or get a glimpse of it within this lifetime. At such moments, we are left speechless, filled with wonder, and a stun that does not disturb; the stun that wakes up one part of our persona we had been unaware of.

The emotional state made up of wonder and courage is not a grey area between being happy or sad. It is *above* the two states. It is a bit different, it is *dramatic*.

Recall your childhood and the giant wheel at the moment of transfer. How much there is to wonder! The cycle of going up and coming down seems so difficult, yet everyone is so secure. The ones sitting in the wheel have no control in their hands, yet they feel so elated. People praise their own courage after getting down from the wheel.

The Infinite Wisdom himself receives the souls who have lived a significant life and accepts them like *prasaad*. How can this ever be painful for anyone?

Live a significant life. Transfer has its own charm. When the intended work is done, returning from the journey is a pleasure.

That moment, this moment, and each moment experience the spirit of wonder, experiment, adventure and courage.

Searching within…

1. What is wonder?
2. What is adventure?
3. What is experiment?
4. What is courage?
5. What name will you give to the emotional state made up of these four elements?

27

DROP ATTACHMENT COMPLETELY. WE ALWAYS MAKE PROGRESS IF WE ARE NOT JERKED BY ATTACHMENT AND AVERSION

There's something about death that is comforting. The thought that you could die tomorrow frees you to appreciate your life now.

- Angelina Jolie

There used to be a story in our childhood books. It is a story about an old wealthy woman who was very attached to her gold ornaments. Somehow she saves the gold from her daughters and daughters-in-law. However, she is always anxious that who will get the ornaments after she passes away. This attachment was so intense that within a few hours after transfer, she returned as a dog in the vicinity of her house, and continued to *keep a watch* on her ornaments.

Attachment is the root cause of bondage and downfall – be it the attachment for ornaments, career, family, habits, name and fame or personal qualities. (The feelings of '*I am good'* come from attachment to self and from comparison with others; '*I am good and they are not as good.*')

Being able to control the mind is wisdom.

When the mind controls us, it is attachment.

Attachments block progress. Or worse, they may cause a reverse movement, as it happened with the old lady in the story who got *demoted* to an animal form from a human one. Having got a human life is a big opportunity to make progress.

Attachment is *karma* at the level of intention.

Drop this attachment. Dropping it may be difficult; close your eyes and throw it away. Get rid of it.

The mind that is stuck sucks the strength and speed of consciousness which must travel. It is like a weight tied to the legs. The consciousness gives up and the story continues from the point at which the mind had been stuck. And this can get really *very* complex.

It is a bit chilling for me to write this. Dr Brian Weiss, in one of his books, says that we may not be born equal. Further, to our relief, he writes, though we may not be born equal, we are destined towards equality.

Hence, let us fixate the mind only on what is good for us and others. The Infinite Wisdom knows everything that is good for each of us. It is best if we can leave everything to this Wisdom.

Searching within…

1. Can we sometimes get confused between our passion and attachment?
2. There is a thin line dividing attachment and envy. *I should have this* – this is attachment. *Why has he got it* - this is envy. Our mind is stuck in both the cases. Let us make a list of 4–5 items on which our mind is stuck at this moment.
3. How does one get rid of attachment? There should not be any rejection, disdain, ignoring, less of love and warmth. The need is to rise above everything. Do you have some suggestions on how to achieve this?
4. One has to overcome attachment and at the same time maintain a sense of responsibility. How does it feel to take care of people, objects and projects?
5. After overcoming attachment, in which part of your personality was there a change noticed by you and others around you?

28

Two possibilities beyond our limited intellect: our ignorance (which we could not know or understand) and the truth (which we could not accept)

No one wants to die. Even people who want to go to heaven don't want to die to get there. And yet death is the destination we all share. No one has ever escaped it. Death is very likely the single best invention of Life. It is life's change agent. It clears out the old to make way for the new.

- Steve Jobs

In ancient literature, there is a simple definition of truth: the truth is that which does not change with time.

In this fast changing world, we are perhaps facing falsehood so explicitly for the first time. Here, everything, every value, every meaning is changing at the blink of our eyes, at the spur of the moment. Perhaps this is the reason we are so anxious, perturbed, scared, and desperate. We have distanced away from the truth, and we need to accept it.

Psychology refers to the phenomenon called the Dunning Kruger Effect. This happens when an ignorant person feels he knows it all and a wise person feels he has to go a long way on the path of learning and acquiring perfection.

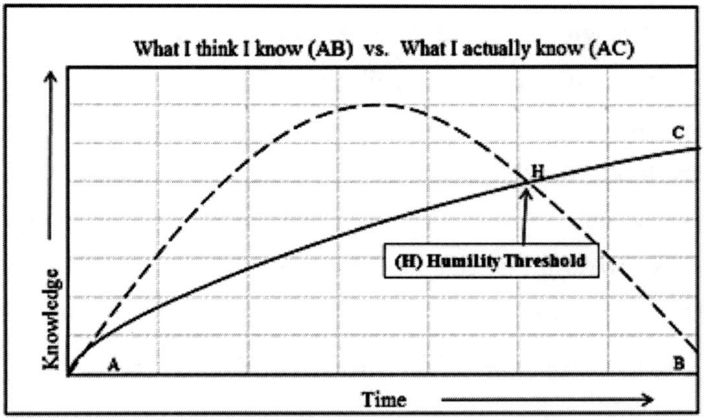

We want to feel that we know many things, rather most things. And this symbolises our ignorance. Perhaps there is a phenomenon (or many) that science has not yet been able to explore or explain. For example; there was a time we did not know about the force of gravity, not even that word. Was gravity, the natural power not present *till* it was explained? What we consider logic or science (evidence-based knowledge) is, in simple words, a description of what is happening out there. It is a description, not the reality or the truth by itself.

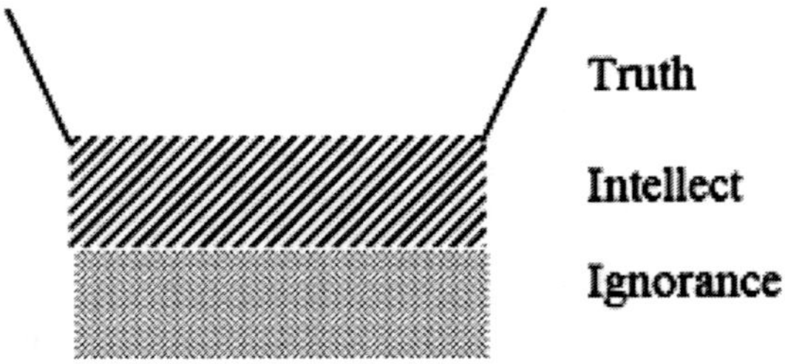

All logic, the bodies of knowledge based on logic, and materialism that usually closely follow knowledge have two norms: (1) the thought or information must be acceptable (through evidence) (2) once a person or scientist has been able to understand a phenomenon, he should be able to write or present his insight in an explainable and comprehendible manner for others to read and discuss. If these two conditions are not satisfied, then the idea will face ridicule and rejection, or both.

And it is a matter of pride that in spite of this risk, a few courageous people gather their own experiences and new perspectives and present the new possible knowledge to humanity. How do they do that? It happens when we distinguish between 'knowing' and 'understanding'.

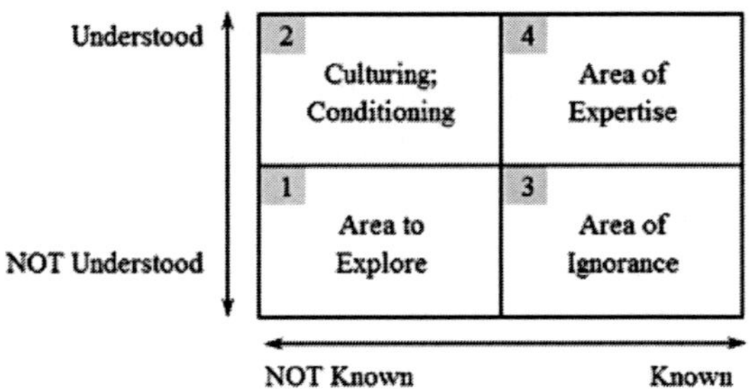

Culturing and **conditioning** happens slowly. For example, we 'understand' that we must respect elders without really 'knowing' or caring to even ask '*why*? On the other extreme, there may be many things we 'know' but do not understand. For example, the importance of a daily health regime. And out of this **ignorance**, we fall into the cycle of inaction. We have **expertise** in quite a few areas, like our professional skills. This leaves us with a few (or many) aspects of 'the totality' which we still need to **explore** – that which we neither know nor understand.

Death, for many thousands of years now, has been associated with all things spooky, creepy, evil, painful and unfortunate. It has been so because hardly have we known, with certainty, answer to the question *what beyond death*. However it is quite possible that, in the times to come, we will *know* it as a 'scientific' fact. We may begin new discussions and accept it as a normal occurrence in the course of the *renewal* of life, explore it as a new school of treatment for chronic or medically incurable symptoms, and establish definite conversations with beings across various planes. And why not? It was only 35 years ago that something like the internet was beyond our wildest imagination and capacity to conceptualise.

Steve Jobs once said, "Death is the destiny we all share, alike." Is a fair understanding of death the 'technology' of the future? Is this understanding a solution for the issues and conflicts that mankind is facing - the conflict between science and abstractness, the conflict between the old generation and the new, the conflict between the ideologies of materialism and purposefulness, the conflict between the haves and have-nots, the conflict between various faiths and sects, and the conflict within a person...

This very thought leaves me at sheer wonder. What are the endless possibilities within the Infinite Wisdom and Infinite Energy – the source to which we are going to return?

Let us simplify the words 'truth' and ignorance' so that we can relate to them.

It is the ego that holds us back and blocks us from accepting the truth.

Ego is equal to weight, the weight of our inner being (the rigidity in thinking, feeling and perceiving). The heavy beings fall down or stay suspended at the lower levels just as it happens at the physical level. When the energies are arranged and rearranged (it happens on a continuous basis), the ones with weight (the ego that has not yet dissolved) will remain at the lower realms called the 'astral' layers. Being at this astral layer is like being stuck in a traffic jam (one is neither at home nor at the destination) – being neither at the physical level nor at the spiritual level. This is the reason we need to shed of the weight called ego.

Having a clear map is the opposite of ignorance. If I reach a new city and ask my friend how to reach M.G. Road, his immediate question would be, "Where are you now?" The ultimate ignorance is when we are unaware of these two facts (i) where we want to reach and (ii) where we are now.

How often we ask these questions with the self? How clear are we on our responses to these two questions? Can anyone else (other than our own inner voice) ever guide us on this? Can we ever succumb to other's guidance on these questions? When we arrive at the state where we let our inner voice guide us, we are free from ignorance.

We were sleeping at 2 a.m. We were sleeping at 3 a.m. We were sleeping even at 5 a.m. But, at some point of time, we woke up – 6 a.m., 7 a.m. or 8 a.m. right? That is how ignorance is. Ignorance is not permanent. We may have been ignorant in the past, we may be ignorant today, and maybe we will remain ignorant for a few more years. But there will come a point in time, a moment, when we will 'wake up'. Remaining ignorant is not our natural quality, being insightful is. It is good if we 'wake up' within this lifetime, now!

Searching within...

1. Just like the human brain decoded the laws of gravitation and made good use of them, will we one day decode all the laws of energy called life and put them to good use.
2. Do we need a system wherein we can discuss with each other in detail and with ease the significant and abstract aspects of living, such as money, sex, life, death, spirituality?
3. We do give due consideration to our physical-biological-social needs. Do we also have a few spiritual needs? If yes, what are they?
4. What is the difference and relationship between education, religion and spirituality?
5. Is one human life sufficient to understand it all?

29

HAVING DONE THIS/WHILE DOING THIS, IF I GET TRANSFERRED, WHAT WILL BE THE RESULT/IMPACT? LET THIS THOUGHT GUIDE TIME UTILISATION

"*I'm going to live till I die.*

- Frank Sinatra

What remains? In the perpetuity of this life and beyond, two elements are unchangeable – time and consciousness. Both are with us today and they will always be available.

Make good use of them. Whatever work (intention, thoughts, decisions, words and actions) you undertake, think about its far-reaching outcome. It is not rocket science.

Make good use of time and energy. Enjoy life and the cycle of lives with composure, grace, and inner beauty.

It is said that the truth and purpose of life is disclosed to man in three ways: (1) need to lead life with a severe physical trouble (2) experiencing death and returning to life (NDE) and (3) through meditation and self-probing.

30

Departure and Enlightenment: What is the Difference?

Enlightenment must come little by little, otherwise it would overwhelm...

- Idries Shah

Is this a good question to think about or discuss?

Every spiritual text and preaching, regardless of faith, place and period of origin, at some stage talks about some kind of 'light within'. Spiritual texts urge you to seek it. They guarantee that it is within you.

Is this light so universal that everyone seems to agree on this one phenomenon?

I don't really know. I feel that all that people talk and write about (including this book) is *their* way of expressing in their own (limited) way. It is like this: when a family goes out on a picnic, each of the family members describes his excitement and experience in his own different way.

Experience is but a small, very small, fraction of the Total Truth. And expression is expression of Truth, not The Truth by itself. Rene Magritte gave this title to one of his paintings - *Ceci n'est pas une pipe* (This is not a pipe).* This explains the point beautifully. What is, is.

If all of them or most of them talk about some light, it cannot be fallacious.

The realisation of the light within, the arrival of more such light and man's efforts to preserve, cherish and guard this feeling and experience is enlightenment. The departure of this light from the body is ***transfer***.

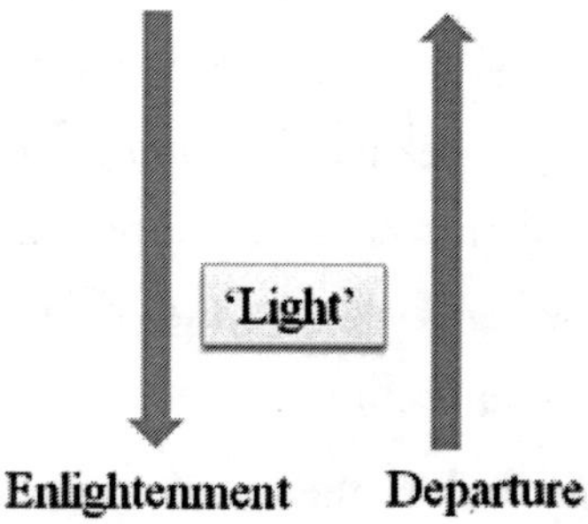

---

* Image source: http://upload.wikimedia.org/wikipedia/en/b/b9/MagrittePipe.jpg accessed March 8, 2015. Translation added by author using some common software.

What is this light? To understand this we need to understand what consciousness is. To do that, let us solve this puzzle. *What is the difference between the mind, the spirit, the soul and the consciousness?* These four terms are usually used as substitutes for each other. But we need to draw a distinction. And here it is. (The textual description below is to only facilitate comprehension; one needs to personally experience it.)

The mind: The nature of the mind is desperation, restlessness (or dullness) and instability. It constantly moves from one point to another point of interest (most of them being sensual in nature, restless for pleasure ***now***). (However, after systematically curing, the same mind can become enormous resource for healing psycho-somatic complications that give rise to number of diseases and relationship problems.)

The spirit: The spirit, on the other hand, is constantly seeking. Its nature is to seek. Many times you may have noticed that you are seeking something. Maybe that is not clear to you, but when *seeking* is happening, the spirit is at work. It is at a higher level than that of the mind. It is the enquiring mode of our being.

The Soul: The soul is the state characterised by love, peace and contentment. It also has the quality of making non-judgemental observations. Unlike the spirit, our anxiety to seek something has reached a halt. Detachment is yet another quality of the soul.

Consciousness: The characteristic qualities of consciousness are purity, energy, constant pulsation, perpetual flow and beauty. This form of 'energy' is not what we usually understand by the term energy: light, electricity, heat, gravity or magnetism. The terms 'energy' and 'light' here are used to describe consciousness because these are words closest to our current capacity to express and understand. (We seek to express and understand through words, don't we? However, words have a limit. By the way, where did the words come from?)

With this working description, I am sure we can figure out quite easily what level one is operating from. People move up from being ignorant and desperate (mind) to being sincere seekers (spirit), to being at peace (soul), and finally reaching the state of selfless action-fullness (consciousness, the state of being thoroughly engaged in selfless action). In terms of purity, the spirit is purer than the mind, the soul is purer than the spirit, and the consciousness is the purest of them all.

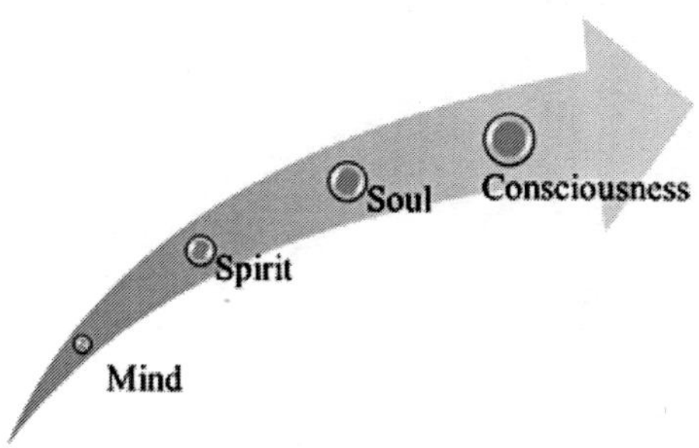

That 'light' is nothing but consciousness. When this 'light' circulates within the body, and more of it arrives from beyond, it is likely that we will neither have fear of death nor waste life. We will be active and full of pure energy.

Believe. Belief always precedes science. Do you recall what Galileo said about the Earth circling the Sun (and the treatment he received from the community)? His belief was ultimately proven scientifically. Nature does not wait for a prior scientific 'approval' or 'acceptance'. Nature constantly moves on. Science is but a study of nature. One can be with nature (having total belief) or with science. What we are unable to believe and accept today, once proven tomorrow becomes science.

31

WHY DO WE LEAD A SKETCHY LIFE?

The quest for peace begins in the home, in the school and in the workplace.

- Silvia Cartwright

No rational person will say 'yes' to this question: *Do you want to lead a sketchy, half-hearted, and insignificant life?* Yet, why do we end up leading a life that is precisely the same – sketchy, half-hearted, and insignificant?

Here is a series of questions and answers that offers some clarity:

Why don't we live the life of full potential?

Because we run away from the truth. There is one subtle spark that tells us what to make of this one life. It points us towards the purpose of life but we ignore it.

Do we really ignore? Why, after all?

We nearly ignore or smother it because we are scared of the truth.

That sounds strange. Why should one blow out one's own calling and voice?

Because if we heed to it, it calls for a lot of work. Tonnes of it, maybe for the entire lifetime. It may even involve hardship. That is why we run away from it.

But you said we run away from the truth. How are the two – truth and purpose of life – connected?

We think of the truth as something limited to speaking. However, there are four dimensions to truth. They are:

- Realising the truth
- Facing the truth
- Being the truth and
- Expressing the truth

We run away right at the first stage, that of realising.

By the way, what is truth?

That which never changes is the truth. Time and place do not have any impact on it.

Sitting in the same place, we notice different things. Truth emerges when we see things differently. And, for that matter, each of us has our own truth.

What then is the purpose of life, one that does not change?

Picking up subtle lessons (refer session 12) from the circumstances that life presents – this is the only purpose of life. And this learning is not intellectual or academic around the brain processes but is at the level of the conscience.

More precisely, though we call it learning, it is actually a process of 'purification' and 'advancement' of the consciousness.

This truth (the purpose of life) is subtle but firm. Till this purpose is accomplished, life hasn't been fully lived.

Can you explain the four dimensions of truth a little more?

Realising the truth is about connecting with your own self. It is possible only through an honest long dialogue with the self. The thin inner voice will remind us time and again that there is a specific *karma* that only you can do so well and it will benefit the rest of the humanity and the surroundings. You will either naturally have all the talent and resources required for it or course of events and circumstances will bring the required resources closer to you. However, in spite of realising this at some point of time in life, we may feel like running away from it. We may run away either because we feel scared (of the volume of work involved) or unprepared. That is where facing the truth comes in.

Facing the truth involves action: action on the face of feeling scared and unprepared. Many skills and resources will be endowed to you when you gain momentum, when your action has been based on faith. Faith that you are in safe hands… Only people with faith will have the courage to face the truth.

Being the truth is being in singleness: oneness in intention, thoughts, words and actions.

We all know that expressing the truth is, to some degree, in saying and writing and also in what people understand from the way we 'broadcast' it non-verbally.

How can we realise the truth faster?

There is a book titled *My Experiments with Truth*. All of us need to experiment with the truth. We can 'experiment' by indulging in life, by engaging well with 'action'. The clarity about *what is it that I can uniquely do or contribute* will emerge from doing this and doing that, not from thinking and idly waiting for that grand idea to appear first. There are two parallel approaches to it: observation and understanding. You may think of these two as two legs for reaching the truth faster.

Observe more than what meets the pair of eyes. One needs to be sensitive and empathetic to *really* observe. It involves observing the self too. Good observation is one that begins with a good question and leads to another good question.

Questions help us expand our understanding. It is said that "when He wants to punish, He first takes away the understanding." Being able to understand is a gifted ability instilled inside us.

And there are not too many truths. As few as they may be, the 'moments of truth' are the turning points of life. Realising the truth brings qualitative change in the way we think, plan, take decisions, and live.

But this seems to be so abstract, confusing and philosophical. Or; am I too young now to think like this?

Let us get it right. Truth and purposefulness are the tools for today's lifestyle, not a goal really.

We may agree with the 'purpose' part quickly because we can correlate the 'purpose' with 'accomplishments'. The Truth requires some explanation. Here it is.

Truth is not really a virtue, it is a tool. Think about it. When we know the truth, we will be able to make the right decisions. Isn't a doctor's prescription likely to go wrong if the patient did not tell him all the truth? Won't a production manager end up taking the incorrect decision if all the facts were not known to him?

We get confused between truth, honesty and integrity. Honesty and integrity are dependent on us. Honesty is the outer behaviour and integrity is the set of values that drive us. However, truth is always independent.

Truth and orientation of life around the truth is not a virtue. It is not a noble quality to be acquired only at old age. It is a tool, a tool for leading a significant life in the professional as well as social capacity. Experimenting with the truth and designing life around it is the way to establish our own brand, i.e., oneness in the way we really are and the way others know us. It is a 'secret sauce' for professional mastery. The sooner we make a beginning, the better it is.

By the way, let me reiterate. Spirituality is grossly misunderstood whereas it is straight and simple. What nutrition is to the body, what education is to the profession, spirituality is to personal growth. Without personal growth, anyone is bound to feel confused or frustrated at some point of time or other, sooner or later.

We also have a tendency to keep it 'pending' for old age. My proposal is: what if spiritual practices delay ageing? Understand spirituality well. Spirituality has nothing to do with idealism, philosophy, region or religion. It is all about developing the internal apparatus (software) to work through the *cause and effect*. It is very scientific. Spirituality helps us overcome duality and confusion faster than any other educational system.

So, is the education we get inadequate? How?

Let us first understand two simple words: knowledge and awareness. If I drop a glass bowl, it will hit the floor. Many of us ***'know'*** it **intellectually** (scientifically, the 'cause' is the force of gravitation). On the other hand, there are many who are ***'aware'*** of this **intuitively** by virtue of (i) common sense or (ii) engaging and experience or (iii) an inner voice telling them so. Can we reject, discard or negate this awareness? Does it not work? Is it usually wrong? No, it does work. We may only ignore it (and we may do it well). This applies not only to the dropping of a glass bowl, but also to many other spheres and situations.

Now, coming to the question about education. The formal education we receive is largely designed to develop our intellect (concepts, reasoning, logic, theory) not our intuitive apparatus and we should not expect it to do so. Intuitive abilities (foresight, managing emotions, judgment, clarity, creativity, and, yes, even humour) develop quite differently: through observation, imagination, and reflection, shadowing and actively engaging in self-initiated learning in non-formal ways.

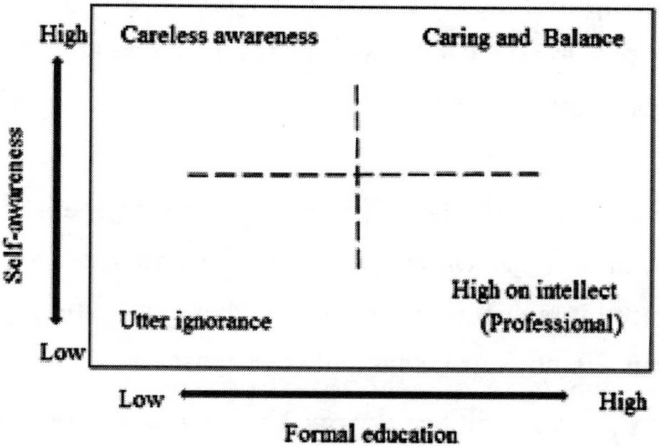

Formal education and non-formal education thus have two distinguishable functions. Comparing the two in any way is like comparing a water purifier to a washing machine. For a normal full life, both are required. We cannot and should not swap one for another. Those of us who can strike a good balance between formal education and non-formal education will be in the most advantageous position.

We talked about having a fear of truth. What is the remedy for this?

The weak feels the fear. I am saying this intuitively, not intellectually.

What is that which feels the fear, our brain or our heart?

Unfortunately, it is our own soul; the soul that was never fed and nourished sufficiently. No, let me explain it properly. It is not the soul that feels the fear, but it is THE one that has all that it takes to manoeuvre through fear. But if it is suppressed, suffocated and ignored, it will become susceptible to fear. Feed it well, guard it well and it will help you overcome all the fear you may face at various stages of life.

By the way, the term 'heart' you used is generic. I am sure you will get clarity on the four components of this software by referring to session 30 where we distinguished the four - mind, spirit, soul and consciousness.

When / how will we know that we are leading a significant life?

When the very question of life and living become secondary and when we get dispassionate about the outcome (because in some ways it is not in our hands) yet passionate about (or rather connected with) working and the work getting done through us, it is then that we get the real fizz of what the 'significant life' has to offer: ultimate joy, contentment and peace. Hence, don't care for 'significance'; rather, watch out if you are experiencing the joy, contentment and peace.

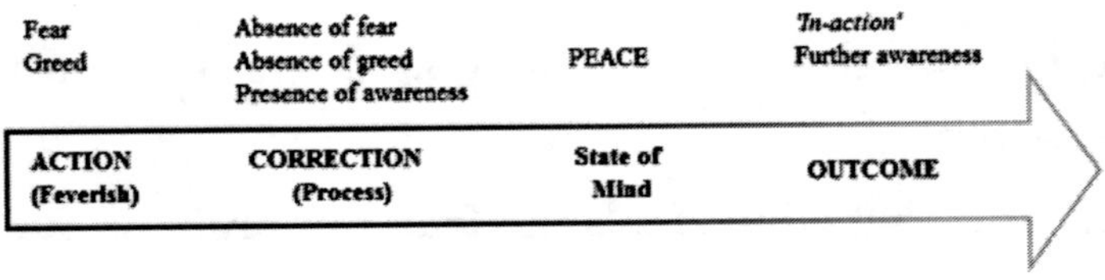

Only when fear disappears, peace prevails. Apart from the absence of fear, emergence of peace also requires absence of greed and presence of awareness. Like height is to the body, peace is to the mind; that is, it cannot be attained instantly. Peace thus arrived never yields inaction, it always is *in action*.

Searching within...

1. Did I discover that some of these questions were mine too but never realised it? Did I get the answers here?
2. Did this discussion stir up some questions in my mind but they have not been discussed here?
3. What is my truth?
4. What is it that I want my truth to be?

32

LIFE: TWO VICIOUS CYCLES AND THREE QUESTIONS

> *Death is a challenge. It tells us not to waste time. It tells us to tell each other right now that we love each other.*
>
> **- Leo Buscaglia**

If we step back and watch, we will find that our life goes round and round within two vicious cycles: 'I-me-mine' and 'no-want-am-cannot'. It is worth analysing once how a large portion of our words and thoughts are caught in these two limitations.

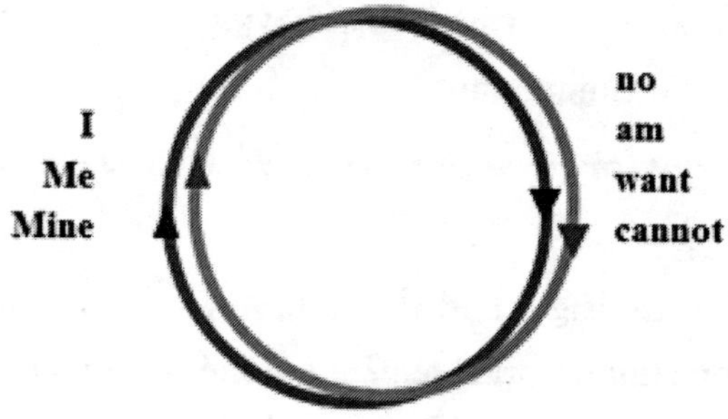

Do think about it and also discuss in the Significance Group.

We almost lose our entire life caught in these two cycles. Would you like to know what our mindset is at the last moment?

Matthew O'Reilly had given a fine 6-minute talk at TED (New York) in 2014. O'Reilly is an emergency medical technician. His job involves, day-in and day-out, dealing with patients who have suffered fatal accidents. Many of these patients ask him: *Am I going to die today?*

In the initial part of his career O'Reilly used to console them or avoid the question. However, one day he simply said 'yes' to a patient who really had no chance of survival. The response of that patient was unexpected and surprising. He accepted this information with grace and composure. The patient expressed only one sorrow. *Alas! I should have given more time and expressed more of my affection for my dear ones.*

O'Reilly, based on his observations, classifies the state of mind at 'those moments' into three types:

1. **Feeling of guilt** for not having done something that was important
2. **Urge for remembrance**: Will others remember me?
3. **Enquiring:** Did I waste my life not doing something worthwhile? This one is the most soul-touching, says O'Reilly, and yes, I agree.

O'Reilly [*] shares an incident of a single mother who was filled with regrets in her last moments for having *simply wasted* her life. After talking with her, O'Reilly learnt that she had adopted two children who were now grown up and were receiving medical education. She had touched two lives positively.

In a way, on deeper analysis, these three questions indicate to one: *What did I do?* (What did I do that was important, that added some value to others, for which people will remember me?)

We need to conscientiously do something meaningful so that we are able to provide answers to ourselves one day.

Pause for a moment and consider this: these questions might be on our mind more intermittently, not only at the last moments. Perhaps we avoid or ignore them.

1. Am I overdoing the 'urgent' at the cost of the 'important'?
2. How will people remember me (what is my image)?
3. What can I do that amounts to *meaning*?

There is only one strategy to break away from these vicious cycles of 'I-me-mine' and 'no-want-am-cannot': adopting a firm and forceful decision built around values. We need to

---

* http://www.ted.com/talks/matthew_o_reilly_am_i_dying_the_honest_answer - as accessed on 19 February, 2015

make up our mind once for all and get down to our 'original' form (a personality characterised by a combination of intense, daring, non-compromising and no-nonsense attitudes). When we reach this form, the joy and zeal in life will be of incredibly *different* quality.

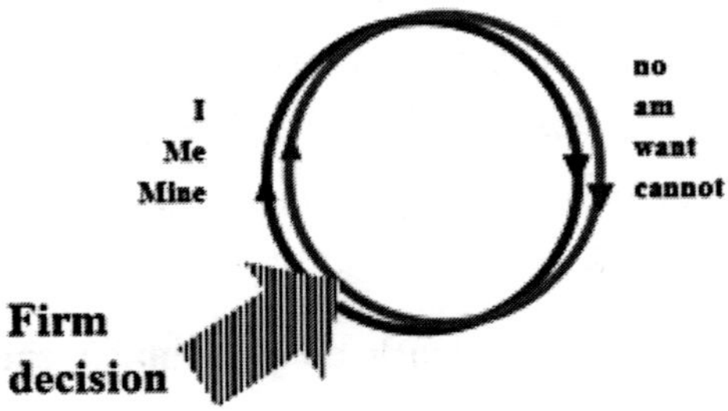

We have a tendency to be on either of the two extremes: hate, guilt, or non-acceptance of our self or too much love for our self.

One of the subtle lessons of life is to develop a well-carved self-fullness. This deserves some discussion.

We know of two extremes of 'selfness' – one is 'selfishness' and the other is 'selflessness'. The first is bad and the latter is good. There is another kind of 'self-ness' that is equally unhelpful. I call it 'self-less-ness' – a state of lack of self-respect, self-esteem and self-acceptance. (Please review the illustration below.)

We usually cannot jump from self-less-ness to self-lessness. Being aware of *who you are* and *what you are here for* requires discovery. This discovery is possible only by 'living' this life. Only after this awareness arises and only after operating from this awareness for a sufficiently long time, can we reach the state of self-fullness. Arriving at this level imparts the **lessons** we intended to learn while assuming this life as well as the subtle **purpose** of life that we did not know so far.

Freedom	**Selflessness** (Spirit of service / Purposefullness)	
Transition	**Self-like-ness** (Here-&-Now, Joy, Contentment)	**Self-full-ness** (Awareness of *who am I* and *what am I here for*)
Stuck	**Selfish-ness** (I / me / mine)	**Self-less-ness** (Rejection / Guilt / Non-acceptance for self)

To put it in simpler words, we have two words 'childish' and 'childlike' with negative and positive connotations, respectively. Similarly, 'selfish' and 'self-like' have negative and positive connotations, respectively. The day we become 'like the self' that really **is**, the joy and passing of moments will not be dependent on each other.

Searching within...

1. Am I caught in one or both the vicious cycles?
2. Think through and list some of your work, gestures, or words that uplifted others and touched them positively, even in the most minor way.
3. Does it (or, should it always) take a *stun* to realize value of life, usefulness of life, or purpose of life?
4. Write or speak into a camera or audio-recorder about the story of your life – circumstances you came from, the values you inherited, the ambitions you had at various points of life, the obstacles and obstructions you faced in various stages, the corrections you made in yourself, how you overcame situations, what happened at the end, what have been your contributions, and what were the lessons you picked up from these situations. Write or record one chapter for each of the above.
5. What is your one secret for good living or a message for others?

33

How does transformation occur?

When we quit thinking primarily about ourselves and our own self-preservation, we undergo a truly heroic transformation of consciousness.

- Joseph Campbell

How does transformation happen? A life built around morals, values and purpose cannot be enforced through constitutional and legal systems. It can be, to some degree if at all, emphasised through professional education, corporate ethics, and a code of conduct, credo or norms. Morals and values and a life built around morals and values can effectively be revived through one of these three ways: emotionally, reflectively and individually.

- How does transformation work emotionally? It is simple. Reaching out to someone and saying these few words with utmost sincerity, loving care, encouragement and positive challenge: *Bro, it has been enough*. These few words can do much more than big inspirational speeches and self-help books.

From so-called intense forms of criminal waste (corruption, crime and aggression) to mild, day-to-day temptations (stealing, bullying, blame, gossip, back-biting), none of these can be controlled through legal and social framework alone; someone has to touch these people at the level of the conscience and emotions.

- Emotions are the seat of all actions. All decisions arise from a mix of rational and emotional thinking. Legal systems can punish them (this is sometimes required too), but cannot change them. The word *bro* can do more than judicial, educational, political, or inauthentic spiritual systems. In most cases, deep within at a corner of their heart somewhere, people know *it is enough*, but, like a child, they are waiting for someone to extend their hands and help them out.
- How do reflections work? Only when we have a **system** where a person can reflect, enter into a dialogue with the self, and stay within the process for as long as it may take (sometimes this process of self-enquiry can be *really* long, it may not throw up an answer instantly). It can even be painful. It may not lead to an answer one had expected. Only when one reaches his own realisation (that there is something wrong with what he is doing and there *is* a need for course-correction and change), there will be a stable and meaningful transformation.

- Or one day, an individual may simply decide to change. He simply takes an active decision. Maybe he observed others, maybe he planned and reached such a decision. It is a natural course of his thinking. He did not have a long dialogue with himself, he was not particularly in any trouble or desperate situation as such. He simply decided to change.

A person changes when (a) someone emotionally inspires or challenges him, touches his sense of being (b) reflectively enquires within himself and (c) individually decides for himself.

You may have now noticed that this book has been designed to help us enquire within (change reflectively) or reach a decision (change individually). The hope is that some of us take up the task of reaching out to more people emotionally and say those magic words: *Bro, enough.* That is when we can expect to have a decline in emotional pollution, a cleaner society, and a cleaner set of systems – family, education, administration, economy, judiciary, media and health.

Searching within...

1. Will it not be beautiful if we transform within this lifetime, and if we can be instrumental in bringing a positive transformation in the lives of a few others?
2. Am I even able to comprehend the meaning and significance of 'change' or 'transformation'? Can I see the 'possibilities' hidden inside transformation?
3. Can I realise the need for transformation? Can I realise the beauty of transformation?

34

WHAT IS THE *BIG IDEA*?

It takes an idea to change the world. It takes a word to change a person.

- Anonymous

So what is the big idea, as they say it in TED, *worth spreading?* The big idea is that we need to master the art of managing and overcoming *fear* for the growth of human community.

About 3–4 decades ago, we almost *re-discovered* that *stress* (or, to be more precise, the excessive, dysfunctional part of stress) was responsible for eroding our potential and efficiency. To a great degree, we also now know the cure for stress - meditation, yoga and *pranayama* (yogic breathing). We had discovered it as a *knowledge* long, long ago; we need to, however, discover it individually as a *personal experience*. This discovery has certainly made enormous contribution to the human development.

The next phase of human development will be characterised by our ability to manage and overcome fear.

Depending only on meditation to overcome fear may not work. In meditation we simply observe the thoughts and allow them to pass by. However the thoughts that get stuck; or the ones we get stuck with, require analysis. These thoughts could be root cause of fear, as well as once tackled, a gateway to new possibilities. Questions are tools for such reflective self-probing. This is best done in a meditative mode. ('Priming', a form of affirmation, may be helpful for managing fear, but only partly).

The true and complete cure for fear is in two big A's: awareness and action.

Awareness of two kinds: First, the root cause of fear (recognising the source, be it humiliation, health, finances, reputation, public-speaking, failure-success or whatever else). Once this awareness arises, we need to artfully, accept it as well as reject it, simultaneously. Secondly, we need to be aware of the Self, the nature, qualities and strengths of the *energy* layer or the *software* layer of our being.

Action; staying in an active mode all the time, engaged in a meaningful task; works because the fear causes a kind of contraction and withdrawal, together resulting in inaction; symptoms just the opposite of nature of our consciousness: expansion, pulsation and action. Action-orientation of this kind arises from space of depth and peacefulness rather than aggression, arrogance and hormones of immaturity; action-orientation which is not hyperactivity or being noisy.

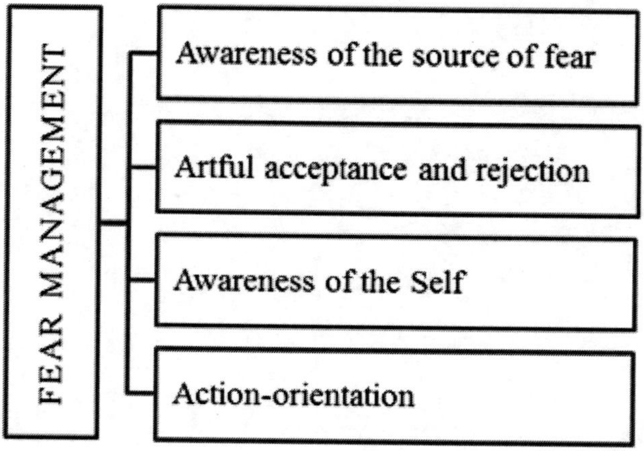

Using this technique, the antidote for our individual and collective fear, we the human community, stand at threshold of the next level of our potential.

In conclusion

- All of us, who are making personal, professional, social and intellectual progress, at some point of time develop an urge for finding the meaning and purpose of this life.
- In most cases, the meaning of life is in doing something significant for others. It is well beyond the 'I-me-mine' circle.
- A normal course of routine (education, society and profession) does not offer the circumstances in which we search for one such purpose. Prescriptions like *follow your passion* may prove futile because we are, as if blind-folded to subscribe to standard 'success patterns' - collecting the indicators: degrees, gadgets, car, house and life-partner. Everyone says 'lead a purposeful life' but no one explains how it is done.
- However, intense and unceasing enquiry within and severe circumstances can throw light on the purpose of life.
- Not having led a life of purpose may result in regret and other symptoms of life that did not fully bloom. Feelings of regret, guilt, having lost the chance to do good, and not having given and received sufficient

love - these are symptoms of life that could not bloom to its fullest. It is even more regretful if these symptoms remain undiscovered.

- We can quickly draw 'lessons' from others' experiences, explanations and research on near-death-experience. (We have always been doing so in all the other walks of life; entire science is someone else's experience).
- In most cases, NDE has helped people experience inexplicable love, peace and clarity on the purposefulness of life.
- Understanding death as an inescapable part of one's lifecycle can be the science of the future. It can fast-forward our personal life philosophies and plans, helping us reorganise our time and activities around specific values, concerns and purposes.
- After freedom from unproductive stress, the next big thing in human development could be freedom from fear.

Whenever we redefine our values and value-systems, it may take an entire generation or two to establish the transition and the envisaged positive effect to manifest. This book pins hope on the young, the ones young at heart and young at mind; on ones who are not *stuck*. I am sure I can count every reader in.

Searching within...

1. Most people need help. Casually say to five people '*happy departures, moment to moment*'. Offer very brief explanation only if they need help to decipher this bunch of words. Notice key ideas and words in their responses. Later, write down their reactions here.

APPENDIX

1. Read these books too

1. *The Choice* — Og Mandino
2. *Theory of Karma* — Heeerabhai Thakkar
3. *Many Lives, Many Masters** — Dr Brian Weiss
4. *Messages from Masters** — Dr Brian Weiss
5. *Journey of Souls: Case Studies of Life Between Lives** – Michael Newton Ph. D
6. *Proof of Heaven: A Neurosurgeon's Journey into the Afterlife** — Dr Eben Alexander
7. *Laws of the Spirit World* — Khorshed Bhavnagri
8. Breath and death have nothing to do with faith and belief. With an open mind and with someone's help, if we can explore the book or commentary titled *Kathopanishad*, let me assure, we will venture into a wealth of insight, 'known' since pre-modern times, about the phenomenon and processes around and beyond what we call 'transfer' now,

-----

[*] These books are recommended also for medical practitioners, psychotherapists, and counsellors.

2. A few ideas for a significant life

- Make a beginning at home. We keep hurting our own people, sometimes knowingly and sometimes unintentionally. Accept them unconditionally. There is no need to make a noise about it. Peacefully and quietly, give respect and space to everyone. Speak to them cordially, treat them well. My experience with my own son that I shared in session 12 in this book indicates just the reverse of what we believe: that we raise our children: *children raise us*. Take an honest deep look at how we are handling and treating others. There is always scope for some improvement.
- Caring for hygiene and the beauty of surroundings.
- Before starting to eat, feel for the farmer. *Let the farmer's family be happy*.
- Control the desperation and urge to criticise or blame someone.
- Spend two hours a week to teach someone or help them learn.
- Send positive vibrations to purify the surroundings by gentle chanting. This is a very scientific and proven ancient system. The effect will be better if this is done collectively, especially in the evening (around 7 p.m.). Do this at least for three minutes (wherever we are, it is not essential to gather at one place). The resonance generated from collective chants is good for children and for the flora and fauna around.

- Give away old books, clothes, toys, electronic gadgets, bicycles and tools to those who can use it. Hoarded things cause obstacles to the flow of energy. When people get something that they can use, they will simply bless you.
- Set aside two or three days exclusively every year for giving services at an orphanage, old-age home, hospital, school, church, religious place, or an NGO.
- Join congregations with other faiths and communities, have respectful small chit-chats across these man-made, mental barriers.
- Sponsor school kits, fees or training of people.
- Help a person or family develop a narrative (or a credo) or a strategy for career and future.
- Help each other in reducing our usage of 'I-me-mine'
- Honestly appreciate someone.
- Take up a local micro-project in your area of interest such as:
  - ✓ Education
  - ✓ Anti-addiction
  - ✓ Hygiene and cleanliness
  - ✓ Health
  - ✓ Good governance
  - ✓ Environment and ecology
  - ✓ Child development

- ✓ Parenting
- ✓ Farming, agriculture
- ✓ Nature and animal care
- ✓ Technology
- ✓ Creativity, arts, literature, music, cooking
- ✓ Nutrition
- ✓ Respect and dignity for all
- ✓ Life values
- ✓ Youth, productivity, entrepreneurship
- ✓ Writing, media, journalism
- ✓ Peace, social integration and harmony
- ✓ Housing, quality of life
- ✓ Research and decoding unnecessary complexities in various systems
- ✓ Speaking, mentoring, hand-holding, counselling

This list may trigger your thoughts to search for other possibilities. The underlying spirit is this: plant some seeds where there is not a particle of 'I-me-mine'.

My favourite idea to pursue: __________

Upcoming books and MOOC (Mass Online Open Courses) PROJECTS BY THE SAME AUTHOR

Career Management in Knowledge Society: Text & Action Career and career strategies redefined for the context we are living in now, packed with techniques and illustrations and the author's own uncanny style of extensive, insightful and end-to-end research. In addition to well-researched inputs, the book presents the 4Q model for soft-skill development and Communication 2.0 that youngsters, trainers and employers will find equally useful.

CELLS ©: A Mass Online Open Course (MOOC) project so that people can put an end to their struggle with English language learning.

Think About It – The Clarity book: Few words and the way these words are illustrated can bring about a turning point; hence this book.

About Addwit

Addwit (www.addwit.org) is an aggregation platform for online and offline learning units and resources in non-formal education. These resources have been well-researched and perfected to ensure an improvement in the quality of life.